W9-CNL-334

Dr. Ackerman's Book of Cocker Spaniels

LOWELL ACKERMAN DVM

BB-104

8573594

Overleaf: A family of buff Cockers owned by Ellen Passage.

The author has exerted every effort to ensure that medical information mentioned in this book is in accord with current recommendations and practice at the time of publication. However, in view of the ongoing advances in veterinary medicine, the reader is urged to consult with his veterinarian regarding individual health issues.

Photographers: Brad & Lori Dubbs, Christine Filler, Isabelle Francais, Dr. Kerry L. Ketring, Robert Pearcy, Vince Serbin.

The presentation of pet products in this book is strictly for instructive purposes only; it does not constitute an endorsement by the author, publisher, owners of dogs portrayed, or any other contributors.

© 1996 by LOWELL ACKERMAN DVM

Distributed in the UNITED STATES to the Pet Trade by T.F.H. Publications, Inc., One T.F.H. Plaza, Neptune City, NJ 07753; distributed in the UNITED STATES to the Bookstore and Library Trade by National Book Network, Inc. 4720 Boston Way, Lanham MD 20706; in CANADA to the Pet Trade by H & L Pet Supplies Inc., 27 Kingston Crescent, Kitchener, Ontario N2B 2T6; Rolf C. Hagen Inc., 3225 Sartelon St. Laurent-Montreal Quebec H4R 1E8; in CANADA to the Book Trade by Vanwell Publishing Ltd., 1 Northrup Crescent, St. Catharines, Ontario L2M 6P5 ; in ENGLAND by T.F.H. Publications, PO Box 15, Waterlooville PO7 6BQ; in AUSTRALIA AND THE SOUTH PACIFIC by T.F.H. (Australia), Pty. Ltd., Box 149, Brookvale 2100 N.S.W., Australia; in NEW ZEALAND by Brooklands Aquarium Ltd. 5 McGiven Drive, New Plymouth, RD1 New Zealand; in Japan by T.F.H. Publications, Japan—Jiro Tsuda, 10-12-3 Ohjidai, Sakura, Chiba 285, Japan; in SOUTH AFRICA by Lopis (Pty) Ltd., P.O. Box 39127, Booysens, 2016, Johannesburg, South Africa. Published by T.F.H. Publications, Inc.

MANUFACTURED IN THE
UNITED STATES OF AMERICA
BY T.F.H. PUBLICATIONS, INC.

CONTENTS

DEDICATION

To my wonderful wife Susan and my three adorable children Nadia, Rebecca and David.

PREFACE

Keeping your Cocker Spaniel healthy is the most important job that you, as an owner, can do. Whereas there are many books available that deal with breed qualities, conformation and show characteristics, this may be the only book available dedicated entirely to the preventative health care of the Cocker Spaniel. This information has been compiled from a variety of sources and assembled here to provide you with the most up-to-date advice available.

This book will take you through the important stages of selecting your pet, screening it for inherited medical and behavioral problems, meeting its nutritional needs, and seeing that it receives optimal medical care.

So, enjoy the book and use the information to keep your Cocker Spaniel the healthiest it can be for a long, full and rich life.

Lowell Ackerman DVM

BIOGRAPHY

Dr. Lowell Ackerman is a world-renowned veterinary clinician, author, lecturer and radio personality. He is a Diplomate of the American College of Veterinary Dermatology and is a consultant in the fields of dermatology, nutrition and genetics. Dr. Ackerman is the author of 34 books and over 150 book chapters and articles. He also hosts a national radio show on pet health care and moderates a site on the World Wide Web dedicated to pet health care issues (http://www.familyinternet.com/pet/pet-vet.htm).

BREED HISTORY

THE GENESIS OF THE MODERN COCKER SPANIEL

The spaniels represent one of the earliest families of dogs to be intentionally bred. Chaucer refers to "spaynel" as early as 1386. By the 15th century, spaniels were being used to flush out game. Our modern  spaniels can trace their immediate ancestry to the Spanish spaniels, which have since gone extinct. In England, future selective breeding was done to create many different spaniels.

Facing page: Spaniels have been the prized hunters and companions of humankind for centuries.

These dogs came in small, medium, and large and could be divided into land and water varieties.

It is from the "flushing" spaniels that our Cocker Spaniels directly descended. The genealogical trail looks like this. From the Spanish Spaniels came the Field Spaniel, then the Norfolk Spaniel, then the Springer Spaniel, then the English Cocker Spaniel and, finally, our Cocker Spaniel. The Cocker or "cocking" Spaniels were bred primarily for hunting woodcock and other birds. They were bred to be small, hardy and easy to maintain. In 1893, the Kennel Club of England accepted the Cocker Spaniel as a distinct breed.

The American Spaniel Club was organized in 1882 and the membership began selectively breeding to create a divergence in the breed. In 1949, the American Kennel Club granted separate registration for both the American and the English Cocker Spaniel and the links between the two were torn asunder. From 1938 until 1951, and again from 1984 to 1990, the Cocker Spaniel was the most popular breed in America. In 1994, the Cocker Spaniel was the fourth most common breed to be registered with the American Kennel Club.

The smallest of the spaniel breeds, the Cocker Spaniel was bred to be easy to maintain—so easy that it quickly established itself as a dog of the hearth rather than the heath, as Brad and Lori Dubbs' dog shows.

The Cocker Spaniel has reigned as America's most popular dog for two of the last six decades.

MIND & BODY

**PHYSICAL AND BEHAVIORAL TRAITS
OF THE COCKER SPANIEL**

The Cocker Spaniel is a merry little dog, perfectly suited to family life. He has been one of the most popular breeds in America for decades because  he is compact, silky and soft, happy to be active or a couch potato, depending on your mood, and constantly makes friends with one look from his expressive eyes.

Facing page: Your Cocker Spaniel is as happy to be by your side hiking the hills as watching the television.

CONFORMATION AND PHYSICAL CHARACTERISTICS

This is not a book about show dogs, so information here will not deal with the conformation of champions and how to select one. The purpose of this chapter is to provide basic information about the stature of a Cocker Spaniel and qualities of a physical nature.

Clearly, beauty is in the eye of the beholder. And, since standards come and standards go, measuring your dog against some imaginary yardstick does little for you or your dog. Just because your dog isn't a show champion doesn't mean that he or she is any less of a family member. And, just because a dog is a champion doesn't mean that he or she is not a genetic time bomb waiting to go off.

When breeders and those interested in showing Cocker Spaniels are selecting dogs, they are looking for those qualities that match the breed "standard." This standard, however, is of an imaginary Cocker Spaniel, and it changes from time to time and from country to country. Thus, the conformation and physical characteristics that pet owners should concentrate on are somewhat different and much more practical.

Even if your Cocker doesn't measure up to the official standard for the breed, he can still make a wonderful pet.

Cocker Spaniels were originally bred to be small-sized dogs. Some were less than 10 inches at the withers and barely 20 pounds. Eventually they were bred to become progressively larger. Most adult males are 15 inches at the withers and bitches are about an inch smaller.

Cocker Spaniel puppies have lovely tails — unless there is surgical intervention. Be aware that it is not necessary to dock tails in the Cocker Spaniel for the dog to be a purebred. Being a true Cocker Spaniel has to do with genetics, not surgery. For those wanting to indulge, tails and dewclaws tend to be docked when pups are three to five days old. Most veterinary associations and even many breed registries are against altering animals to create an artificial image. Consider carefully your rationale if you decide to have these procedures done.

COAT COLOR, CARE AND CONDITION

There are three "approved" color distinctions of Cocker Spaniels: black; any solid color other than black (ASCOB); and particolor. The second category includes a wide range of hues such as buff, silver, liver, red, and chocolate/tan. Parti-colors have two or more distinct colors and

With their soft coats, compact size and merry dispositions, it's no wonder Cockers are so popular with families.

may be black and white, black, white and tan, red and white, buff and white, liver and white, liver and white with tan, sable and white, and roan.

The genetics of coat color are fairly complex in the Cocker Spaniel and are controlled by four different genes. The solid black color (As) is dominant over buff/yellow (Ay) and black and tan pattern (at). The dominant black gene (B) takes precedence over the recessive liver/chocolate gene (b). The extension gene in its dominant form (E) allows the coat to be black; having two recessives for this gene (ee) forbids the manifestation of black (buff). This is extremely confusing to many breeders because the buff can be created from the agouti allele (Ay) or the double-recessive extension series (ee).

Without becoming geneticists we can still appreciate how the colors occur in the breed with some basic rules. Each pup receives half a set of genes from its mother and father. Genotype refers to the genetic combinations which we can't see (e.g., atatBBEespsp) while phenotype refers to the products we can see (e.g., black and tan with white).

Coat care is extremely important in the Cocker if the fur is allowed to remain long. Daily brushing is advised to control mats, remove dead undercoat, and add sheen to the fur. Most pet Cockers do not require a full show coat, and more practical clips make routine grooming much easier. Cockers have lip folds, and these areas are perfect areas for bacterial infections to form. Regularly clean these folds with a mild antiseptic solution such as chlorhexidine or hydrogen peroxide to help ward off infection.

BEHAVIOR AND PERSONALITY OF THE ACTIVE COCKER SPANIEL

Behavior and personality are two qualities which are hard to standardize within a breed. Although generalizations are difficult to make, most Cocker Spaniels are alert, energetic and people-oriented. They make great working dogs because they do have the capacity to be loyal, determined, watchful, and obedient. However, it is their social nature that makes them want to work with people. This is not the breed to be tied in the backyard or kept in a cage. Whether they are shy or vicious has something to do with their genetics, but also is determined by the socialization and training they receive.

Behavior and personality are incredibly important in dogs, and there seem to be quite evident extremes in the Cocker Spaniel. Because the breed has been so popular for so long, there have been many opportunities for less-than-diligent breeders to create Cockers that were behavioral nightmares. The ideal Cocker Spaniel is neither aggressive, fearful, nor neurotic but rather a loving family member with good self-esteem and acceptance of position in the family pack. Because the Cocker Spaniel is an energetic dog and can cause much damage, it is worth spending the time when selecting a pup to pay attention to any evidence of personality problems. It is also imperative that *all* Cocker Spaniels be obedience trained. Like any dog, they have the potential to be vicious without appropriate training; consider obedience classes mandatory for your sake and that of your dog.

Content to be a couch potato, your Cocker Spaniel still needs his exercise and will thrive with regular romps.

Although many Cocker Spaniels are happy to sleep the day away in bed or on a sofa, most enjoy having a purpose in their day. That makes them excellent working dogs. They need regular exercise and they do appreciate events that involve family members. All Cocker Spaniels should attend obedience classes and they need to learn limits to unacceptable behaviors. A well-loved and well-controlled Cocker Spaniel is certain to be a valued family member.

For pet owners, there are several activities to which your Cocker Spaniel is well suited. They make great walking and jogging partners, and they are also excellent community volunteers. The loyal and loving Cocker Spaniel will also be your personal guard dog if properly trained; aggressiveness and viciousness do not fit into the equation.

For Cocker Spaniel enthusiasts who want to get into more competitive aspects of the dog world, showing, obedience, field trials, hunting and tracking are all activities that can be considered.

SELECTING

**WHAT YOU NEED TO KNOW TO FIND
THE BEST COCKER SPANIEL PUPPY**

Owning the perfect Cocker Spaniel rarely happens by accident. On the other hand, owning a genetic dud is almost always the result of an impulse purchase and

failure to do even basic research. Buying this book is a major step in understanding the situation and making intelligent choices.

Facing page: When considering a Cocker puppy, it's important to choose a sound, healthy dog and not just the first one you see.

16

SOURCES

Recently, a large survey was done to determine whether there were more problems seen in animals adopted from pet stores, breeders, private owners or animal shelters. Somewhat surprisingly, there didn't appear to be any major difference in total number of problems seen from these sources. What was different were the kinds of problems seen in each source. Thus, you can't rely on any one source because there are no standards by which judgments can be made. Most veterinarians will recommend that you select a "good breeder" but there is no way to identify such an individual. A breeder of champion show dogs may also be a breeder of genetic defects.

The best approach is to select a pup from a source that regularly performs genetic screening and has documentation to prove it. If you are intending to be a pet owner, don't worry about whether your pup is show quality. A mark here or there that might disqualify the pup as a show winner has absolutely no impact on its ability to be a loving and healthy pet. Also, the vast majority of dogs will be neutered and not used for breeding anyway. Concentrate on the things that are important.

MEDICAL SCREENING

Whether you are dealing with a breeder, a breed rescue group, a shelter or a pet store, your approach should be the same. You want to identify a Cocker Spaniel that you can live with and screen it for medical and behavioral problems before you make it a permanent family member. If the source you select has not done the important testing needed, make sure they will offer you a health/temperament guarantee before you remove the dog from the premises to have the work done yourself. If this is not acceptable, or they are offering an exchange-only policy, keep moving; this isn't the right place for you to get a dog. As soon as you purchase a Cocker, pup or adult, go to your veterinarian for thorough evaluation and testing.

Select a puppy from someone who has performed genetic screening on his breeding stock.

Conscientious breeders try hard to produce litters of puppies they hope will grow up to be healthy adults.

Pedigree analysis is best left to true enthusiasts, but there are some things that you can do, even as a novice. Inbreeding is to be discouraged so check out your four- or five-generation pedigree and look for names that appear repeatedly. Reputable breeders will usually not allow inbreeding at least three generations back in the puppy's pedigree. Also ask the breeder to provide OFA, GDC and CERF (see below) registration numbers on all ancestors in the pedigree for which testing is done. If there are a lot of gaps, the breeder has some explaining to do.

The screening procedure is easier if you select an older dog.

Animals can be registered for hips and elbows as young as two years of age by the Orthopedic Foundation for Animals (OFA) and by one year of age by Genetic Disease Control (GDC). This is your insurance against hip dysplasia and elbow dysplasia later in life. Although Cocker Spaniels now have a relatively low incidence of these orthopedic problems, it is because of the efforts of conscientious breeders who have been doing the appropriate testing. A verbal testimonial that they've never heard of the condition in their lines is not adequate and probably means they really don't know if they have a problem. Move along.

Evaluation is somewhat more

complicated in the Cocker Spaniel puppy. The PennHip™ procedure can determine risk for developing hip dysplasia in pups as young as 16 weeks of age. For pups younger than that, you should request copies of OFA or GDC registration for both parents. If the parents haven't both been registered, their hip and elbow status should be considered unknown and questionable.

All Cocker Spaniels, regardless of age, should be screened for evidence of von Willebrand's disease. This can be accomplished with a simple blood test.

The incidence is high enough in the breed that there is no excuse for not performing the test.

For animals older than one year of age, your veterinarian will also want to take a blood sample to check for thyroid function in addition to von Willebrand's disease. A heartworm test, urinalysis and evaluation of feces for internal parasites is also indicated. If there are any patches of hair loss, a skin scraping should be taken to determine if the dog has evidence of demodectic mange.

Your veterinarian should also

Cockers can live long, healthy lives if they've been evaluated as clear of hip or elbow dysplasia.

A family portrait. If the parents are sound physically and behaviorally, chances are the puppies will be too.

perform a very thorough ophthalmologic (eye) examination. The most common eye problems in Cocker Spaniels are cataracts, glaucoma and retinal dysplasia. It is best to acquire a pup whose parents have both been screened for heritable eye diseases and certified "clear" by organizations such as CERF (Canine Eye Registration Foundation). If this has been the case, an examination by your veterinarian is probably sufficient and referral to an ophthalmologist is only necessary if recommended by your veterinarian.

BEHAVIORAL SCREENING

Medical screening is important, but don't forget temperament. More dogs are killed each year for behavioral reasons than for all medical problems combined. Temperament testing is a valuable although not infallible tool in the screening process. The reason that temperament is so important is that many dogs are eventually destroyed because they exhibit undesirable behaviors. Although not all behaviors are evident in young pups (e.g., aggression often takes many months to manifest itself), detecting anxious and fearful pups (and avoiding them) can be very important in the selection process. Traits most identifiable in the young pup include fear; excitability; low pain threshold; extreme submission; and noise sensitivity. There are many different techniques available and a complete discussion is beyond the scope of this book.

Pups can be evaluated for temperament as early as seven to eight weeks of age. Some behaviorists, breeders, and trainers recommend objective testing where scores are given in several different categories. Others are more casual about the process since it is only a crude indicator anyway. In general, the evaluation takes place in three stages, by someone the pup has not been exposed to. The testing is not done within 72 hours of vaccination or surgery. First, the pup is observed and handled to determine its sociability. Puppies with obvious undesirable traits such as shyness, overactivity, or uncontrollable biting may turn out to be unsuitable. Second, the desired pup is separated from the others and then observed for how it responds when played with and called. Third, the pup should be stimulated in various ways and responses noted. Suitable activities include lying the pup on its side, grooming it, clipping its nails, gently grasping it around the muzzle and testing its reactions to noise. In a study conducted at the Psychology Department of Colorado State University, it was found that heart rate was a good indicator in this third stage of evaluation. Actually, the study noted the resting heart rate, stimulated the pups with a loud noise and measured how long it took the heart rate to recover to resting levels. Most pups recovered within 36 seconds. Dogs that took considerably longer were more likely to be anxious.

Puppy aptitude tests (PAT) can be given, in which a numerical score is given for eleven different traits, with a "1" representing the most assertive or aggressive expression of a trait and a "6" representing disinterest, independence, or inaction. The traits assessed in the PAT include social attraction to people; following; restraint; social dominance; elevation (lifting off ground by evaluator); retrieve; touch sensitivity; sound sensitivity; prey/chase drive; sta-

There are puppy aptitude tests that measure such traits as attraction to people, dominance, energy level—even touch and sound sensitivity.

Introducing puppies to children and horses will make them less fearful of kids and other animals later in life.

bility; and energy level. Although the tests do not absolutely predict behaviors, they do tend to do well at predicting puppies at behavioral extremes.

ORGANIZATIONS YOU SHOULD KNOW ABOUT

Project TEACH™ (Training and Education in Animal Care and Health) is a voluntary accreditation process for those individuals selling animals to the public. It is administered by Pet Health Initiative, Inc. (PHI) and provides instruction on genetic screening as well as many other aspects of proper pet care. TEACH-accredited sources screen animals for a variety of medical, behavioral and infectious diseases *before* they are sold. Project TEACH™ supports the efforts of registries such as OFA, GDC and CERF and recommends that all animals sold be registered with the appropriate agencies. For more information on Project TEACH™, send a self-addressed stamped envelope to Pet Health Initiative, P.O. Box 12093, Scottsdale, AZ 85267-2093.

The Orthopedic Foundation for Animals (OFA) is a nonprofit organization established in 1966 to collect and disseminate information concerning orthopedic diseases of animals and to es-

Thanks to organizations like the OFA, canine orthopedic diseases will continue to decrease.

tablish control programs to lower the incidence of orthopedic diseases in animals. A registry is maintained for both hip dysplasia and elbow dysplasia. The ultimate purpose of OFA certification is to provide information to dog owners to assist in the selection of good breeding animals; therefore, attempts to get a dysplastic dog certified will only hurt the breed by perpetuation of the disease. For more information contact your veterinarian or the Orthopedic Foundation for Animals, 2300 Nifong Blvd., Columbia, MO 65201.

The Institute for Genetic Disease Control in Animals (GDC) is a nonprofit organization founded in 1990 and maintains an open registry for orthopedic problems but does not compete with OFA. In an open registry like GDC, owners, breeders, veterinarians, and scientists can trace the genetic history of any particular dog once that dog and close relatives have been registered. At the present time, the GDC operates open registries for hip dysplasia, elbow dysplasia, and osteochondrosis. The GDC are currently developing guidelines for registries of Legg-Calve-Perthes disease, craniomandibular osteopathy, and medial patellar luxation. For more information, contact the Institute for Genetic Disease Control in Animals, P.O. Box 222, Davis, CA 95617.

The Canine Eye Registration Foundation (CERF) is an international organization devoted to eliminating hereditary eye diseases from purebred dogs. This organization is similar to OFA, which helps eliminate diseases like hip dysplasia. CERF is a non-profit organization that screens and certifies purebreds as free of heritable eye diseases. Dogs are evaluated by veterinary eye specialists and the findings are then submitted to CERF for documentation. The goal is to identify purebreds without heritable eye problems so they can be used for breeding. Dogs being considered for breeding programs should be screened and certified by CERF on an annual basis since not all problems are evident in puppies. For more information on CERF, write to CERF, SCC-A, Purdue University, West Lafayette, IN 47907.

All puppies deserve to grow up free of crippling diseases, and with proper screening, they can.

FEEDING & NUTRITION

WHAT YOU MUST CONSIDER EVERY DAY TO FEED YOUR COCKER SPANIEL THROUGH HIS LIFETIME

Nutrition is one of the most important aspects of raising a healthy Cocker Spaniel and yet it is often the source of much controversy between breeders, veterinarians, pet owners, and dog food manufacturers. However, most of these arguments have more to do with marketing than with science.

Facing page: Feeding your Cocker right means understanding what's in the food he's eating.

Let's first take a look at dog foods and then determine the needs of our dog. This chapter will concentrate of feeding the pet Cocker Spaniel rather than breeding or working animals.

COMMERCIAL DOG FOODS

Most dog foods are sold based on marketing (i.e., how to make a product appealing to owners while meeting the needs of dogs). Some foods are marketed on the basis of their protein content, others based on a "special" ingredient, and some are sold because they don't contain certain ingredients (e.g., preservatives, soy). We want a dog food that specifically meets our dog's needs, is economical and causes few, if any, problems. Most foods come in dry, semi-moist and canned forms. Some can now be purchased frozen. The "dry" foods are the most economical, contain the least fat and the most preservatives. The canned foods are the most expensive (they're 75 percent water), usually contain the most fat, and have the least preservatives. Semi-moist foods are expensive, high in sugar content and I do not recommend them for any dogs.

When you're selecting a commercial diet, make sure the food has been assessed by feeding trials for a specific life stage, not just by nutrient analysis. This statement is usually located not far from the ingredient label. In the United States, these trials

Puppies have unique nutritional requirements. There are many puppy foods on the market to choose from.

To satisfy a growing puppy's need to chew and play, give him a Nylabone®.

are performed in accordance with American Association of Feed Control Officials (AAFCO) and, in Canada, by the Canadian Veterinary Medical Association. This certification is important because it has been found that dog foods currently on the market that provide only a chemical analysis and calculated values but no feeding trial may not provide adequate nutrition. The feeding trials show that the diets meet minimal, not optimal, standards. However, they are the best tests we currently have.

PUPPY REQUIREMENTS

Soon after pups are born, and certainly within the first 24 hours, they should begin nursing their mother. This provides them with colostrum, which is an antibody-rich milk that helps protect them from infection for their first few months of life. Pups should be allowed to nurse for at least six weeks before they are completely weaned from their mother. Supplemental feeding may be started by as early as three weeks of age.

By two months of age, pups should be fed puppy food. They are now in an important growth phase. Nutritional deficiencies and/or imbalances during this time of life are more devastating that at any other time. Also, this is not the time to overfeed pups or provide them with "performance" rations. Overfeeding Cockers can lead to serious skeletal defects such as osteochondrosis, cervical vertebral instability, and hip dysplasia. Also, the Cocker Spaniel has a tendency towards obesity, so overfeeding is not desirable at any time in life.

Pups should be fed "growth" diets until they are 12 months of age. Cockers also have a tendency towards obesity and, since puppy food tends to be high in calories, some veterinarians may recommend switching to a maintenance diet sooner. Pups will initially need to be fed two to three meals daily until they are 12 months old, then once to twice daily (preferably twice) when they are converted to adult food. Proper growth diets should be selected based on acceptable feeding trials designed for growing pups. If you can't tell by reading the label, ask your veterinarian for feeding advice.

Remember that pups need "balance" in their diets, and avoid the temptation to supplement with protein, vitamins, or minerals. Calcium supplements have been implicated as a cause of bone and cartilage deformity, especially in large-breed puppies. Puppy diets are already heavily fortified with calcium, and supplements tend to unbalance the mineral intake. There is more than adequate proof that these supplements are responsible for many bone deformities seen in these growing dogs.

ADULT DIETS

The goal of feeding adult dogs is one of "maintenance." They have already done the growing they are going to do and are unlikely to have the digestive problems of elderly dogs. In general, dogs can do well on maintenance rations containing predominantly plant or animal-based ingredients as long as that ration has been specifically formulated to meet maintenance level requirements. This contention should be supported by studies performed by the manufacturer in accordance with the AAFCO (American Association of Feed Control Officials). In Canada, these products should be certified by the Canadian Veterinary Medical Association to meet maintenance requirements.

There's nothing wrong with feeding a cereal-based diet to dogs on maintenance rations, and they are the most economical. When comparing maintenance rations, it must be appreciated that these diets must meet the "minimum" requirements for confined dogs, not necessarily optimal levels. Most dogs will benefit when fed diets that contain easily-digested ingredients that provide nutrients at least slightly above minimum requirements. Typically, these foods will be intermediate in price between the most expensive super-premium diets and the cheapest

As your dog ages, her metabolism slows down and her organs function differently, so you'll need to talk to your vet about changing her diet. This is Princess Kahlua Wise.

generic diets. Select only those diets that have been substantiated by feeding trials to meet maintenance requirements, those that contain wholesome ingredients, and those recommended by your veterinarian. Don't select based on price alone, on company advertising, or on total protein content.

GERIATRIC DIETS

Cocker Spaniels are considered elderly when they are about seven years of age, and there are certain changes that occur as dogs age that alter their nutritional requirements. As pets age, their metabolism slows, and this must be accounted for. If maintenance rations are fed in the same amounts while metabolism is slowing, weight gain may result. Obesity is the last

thing one wants to contend with in an elderly pet, since it increases the risk of several other health-related problems. As pets age, most of their organs function not as well as in youth. The digestive system, the liver, pancreas and gallbladder are not functioning at peak effect. The intestines have more difficulty extracting all the nutrients from the food consumed. A gradual decline in kidney function is considered a normal part of aging.

A responsible approach to geriatric nutrition is to realize that degenerative changes are a normal part of aging. Our goal is to minimize the potential damage done by taking this into account while the dog is still well. If we wait until an elderly dog is ill before we change the diet, we have a much harder job.

Elderly dogs need to be treated as individuals. While some benefit from the nutrition found in "senior" diets, others might do better on the highly-digestible puppy and super-premium diets. These latter diets provide an excellent blend of digestibility and amino acid content but, unfortunately, many are higher in salt and phosphorus than the older pet really needs.

Older dogs are also more prone to developing arthritis; therefore, it is important not to

If your Cocker has plenty of energy and a full, shiny coat, he is getting the right nutrients in the right amounts.

overfeed them since obesity puts added stress on the joints. For animals with joint pain, supplementing the diet with fatty acid combinations containing cis-linoleic acid, gamma-linolenic acid and eicosapentaenoic acid can be quite beneficial.

MEDICAL CONDITIONS AND DIET

Obesity is the most common nutritional disease afflicting dogs and cats today, currently exceeding all deficiency-related diseases combined. It is quite common in the Cocker Spaniel. Perhaps the pet food companies have done their jobs too well, but the newer foods are probably much tastier to pets than previous ones and encourage eating. Because many people leave food down all day for free-choice feeding, animals consume

more and gain weight. The incidence of obesity increases with age. It is about twice as common in neutered as in nonneutered animals of either sex and, up to 12 years of age, is more common in females than in males. Recent studies indicate that even moderate obesity can significantly reduce both the quality and the length of an animal's life. Fortunately, it is a situation that can be remedied.

Neutered animals should be fed a nutritionally balanced, reduced-calorie diet that has been specifically formulated for the high-risk, obesity-prone animal. Weight reduction in most animals can be accomplished with a medically supervised program of caloric restriction. This requires a genuine, long-term commitment by the pet owner to alter poor feeding habits and provide adequate exercise. Snacks are also an important part of the equation. Since most biscuit treats are 60-100 calories each, it doesn't take many to add pounds to a frame. Give biscuit treats in moderation and consider alternatives such as carrots, chew toys, high-fiber biscuits, or a nice walk instead of a snack.

It is important to keep in mind that dietary choices can affect the development of orthopedic diseases such as hip dysplasia and osteochondrosis. When feeding a pup at risk, avoid high-calorie diets and try to feed several times a day rather than ad libitum. Sudden growth spurts are to be avoided because they result in joint instability. Recent research has also suggested that the electrolyte balance of the diet may also play a role in the development of hip dysplasia. Rations that had more balance between the positively and negatively charged elements in the diet (e.g., sodium, potassium, chloride) were less likely to promote hip dysplasia in susceptible dogs. Also avoid supplements of calcium, phosphorus and vitamin D, as they can interfere with normal bone and cartilage development. The fact is that calcium levels in the body are carefully regulated by hor-

mones (such as calcitonin and parathormone) as well as vitamin D. Supplementation disturbs this normal regulation and can cause many problems. It has also been shown that calcium supplementation can interfere with the proper absorption of zinc from the intestines. If you really feel the need to supplement your dog, select products such as eicosapentaenoic/gamma-linolenic fatty acid combinations or small amounts of vitamin C.

You can't prevent heart disease in dogs entirely by dietary changes, but there are some things that you can do to help. In addition to selecting a properly formulated diet, nutritional supplements can be useful additions. In the Cocker Spaniel in particular, research has shown that taurine levels have a direct impact on the development of the heart disease known as dilated cardiomyopathy. Some breeds prone to dilated cardiomyopathy have been shown to respond to supplements of coenzyme Q. Until the research has been done, it may be advisable to begin supplementation with both taurine and coenzyme Q10 by two years of age. The accepted dosage for taurine is 500 milligrams twice daily. For coenzyme Q, a dose has not been precisely determined for dogs, but some cardiologists are using doses of 30-90 mg/day. The soft gelatin capsules are preferred and they can be orally administered or punctured and squirted onto the food. This has been shown to improve heart muscle function and may delay the onset of clinical heart disease in susceptible animals.

Fat supplements are probably the most common supplements purchased from pet supply stores. They frequently promise to add luster, gloss, and sheen to the coat, and consequently make dogs look healthy. The only fatty acid that is essential for this purpose is cis-linoleic acid, which is found in flaxseed oil, sunflower seed oil, and safflower oil. Corn oil is a suitable but less effective alternative. Most of the other oils found in retail supplements are high in saturated and monounsaturated fats and are not beneficial for shiny fur or healthy skin. For dogs with seborrhea (seen most commonly in the Cocker Spaniel), allergies, arthritis, high blood pressure (hypertension), high cholesterol, and some heart ailments, other fatty acids may be prescribed by a veterinarian. The important ingredients in these products are gamma-linolenic acid (GLA), eicosapentaenoic acid (EPA), and docosahex-

Avoid feeding supplements of calcium, phosphorous and vitamin D. They can interfere with bone and cartilage development.

These puppies have been weaned off their mother's milk and on to solid food.

aenoic acid (DHA). These products have gentle and natural anti-inflammatory properties. But don't be fooled by imitations. Most retail fatty acid supplements do not contain these functional forms of the essential fatty acids - look for gamma-linolenic acid, eicosapentaenoic acid and docosahexaenoic acid on the label. Most Cockers benefit from these supplements — or at least from daily administration of sunflower or safflower oil. Studies in the Cocker Spaniel have shown these to be effective in managing seborrhea.

Zinc is an important mineral when it comes to immune function and wound healing, but it has some other uses in the Cocker Spaniel. Zinc administration, particularly zinc acetate, can also promote copper excretion from the body. Usually this is not necessary or even desirable, but some Cocker Spaniels have an inherited disease that causes them to store copper in their liver; the result can be chronic hepatitis. Although this copper-induced hepatitis cannot be cured, zinc supplementation can be used as a safe and effective form of therapy.

35

HEALTH

**PREVENTIVE MEDICINE AND HEALTH
CARE FOR YOUR COCKER SPANIEL**

Keeping your Cocker Spaniel healthy requires preventive health care. This is not only the most effective, but the least expensive way to battle illness.

Good preventive care starts even before puppies are born. The dam should be well cared for, vaccinated and free of infections and parasites.

Facing page: Regular visits to your veterinarian go a long way toward keeping your Cocker in fine form.

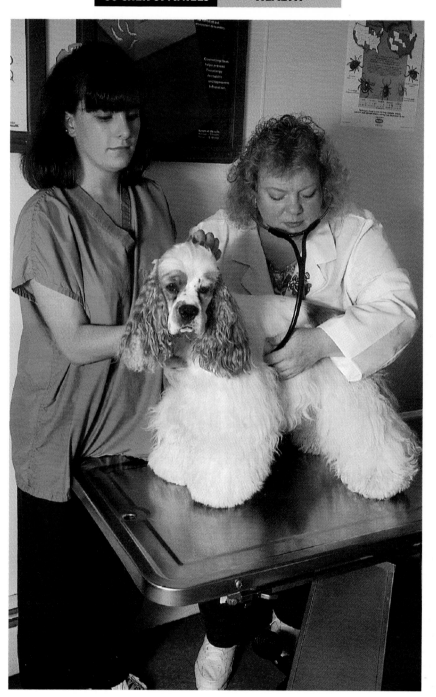

Hopefully, both parents were screened for important genetic diseases (e.g. von Willebrands's disease), registered with the appropriate agencies (e.g., OFA, GDC, CERF), showed no evidence of medical or behavioral problems and were found to be good candidates for breeding. This gives the pup a good start in life. If all has been planned well, the dam will pass on resistance to disease to her pups that will last for the first few months of life. However, the dam can also pass on parasites, infections, genetic diseases and more.

Puppies first visit the veterinarian when they turn six to eight weeks of age.

TWO TO THREE WEEKS OF AGE

By two to three weeks of life, it is usually necessary to start pups on a regimen to control worms. Although dogs benefit from this parasite control, the primary reason for doing this is human health. After whelping, the dam often sheds large numbers of worms even if she tested negative previously. This is because many worms lay dormant in tissues and the stress of delivery causes parasite release and shedding into the environment. Assume that all puppies potentially have worms, because studies have shown that 75 percent do. Thus, we institute worm control

early to protect the people in the house from worms, more than the pups themselves. The deworming is repeated every two to three weeks until your veterinarian feels the condition is under control. Nursing bitches should be treated at the same time because they often shed worms during this time. Only use products recommended by your veterinarian. Over-the-counter parasiticides have been responsible for deaths in pups.

SIX TO TWENTY WEEKS OF AGE

Most puppies are weaned from their mother at six to eight weeks of age. Weaning shouldn't be done too early so that pups have the opportunity to socialize with their littermates and dam. This is important for them to be able to respond to other dogs later in life. There is no reason to rush the weaning process unless the dam can't produce enough milk to feed the pups.

Pups are usually first examined by their veterinarian at six to eight weeks of age, which is when most vaccination schedules commence. If pups are exposed to many other dogs at this young age, veterinarians often opt for vaccinating with inactivated parvovirus at six weeks of age. When exposure isn't a factor, most veterinarians would rather wait to see the pup at eight weeks of age. At this point, they can also do a preliminary dental evaluation to see that all the puppy teeth are coming in

correctly, check to see that the testicles are properly descending in males and that there are no health reasons to prohibit vaccination at this time. Heart murmurs, wandering knee-caps (luxating patellae), juvenile cataracts, persistent pupillary membranes (a congenital eye disease) and hernias are usually evident by this time.

Your veterinarian may also be able to perform temperament testing on the pup by eight weeks of age, or recommend someone to do it for you. Although temperament testing is not completely accurate, it can often predict which pups are most anxious and fearful. Some form of temperament evaluation is im-

A veterinarian can check a young puppy for heart murmurs, juvenile cataracts, hernias and other problems.

Studies have shown that neutering is less stressful in younger dogs — all the more reason to have the procedure done early in your Cocker's life.

portant because behavioral problems account for more animals being euthanized (killed) each year than all medical conditions combined.

Recently, some veterinary hospitals have been recommending neutering pups as early as six to eight weeks of age. A study done at the University of Florida College of Veterinary Medicine over a span of more than four years concluded there was no increase in complications when animals were neutered when less than six months of age. The evaluators also concluded that the surgery appeared to be less stressful when done in young pups.

Most vaccination schedules consist of injections being given at 6—8, 10—12, and 14—16 weeks of age. Ideally, vaccines should not be given closer than

two weeks apart, and three to four weeks seems to be optimal. Each vaccine usually consists of several different viruses (e.g., parvovirus, distemper, parainfluenza, hepatitis) combined into one injection. Coronavirus can be given as a separate vaccination according to this same schedule if pups are at risk. Some veterinarians and breeders advise another parvovirus booster at 18—20 weeks of age. A booster is given for all vaccines at one year of age and annually thereafter. For animals at increased risk of exposure, parvovirus vaccination may be given as often as four times a year. A new vaccine for canine cough (tracheobronchitis) is squirted into the nostrils. It can be given as early as six weeks of age if pups are at risk. Leptospirosis vaccination is given in some geographic areas and likely offers protection for six to eight months. The initial series consists of three to four injections spaced two to three weeks apart, starting as early as ten weeks of age. Rabies vaccine is given as a separate injection at three months of age, then repeated when the pup is one year old, then every one to three years depending up local risk and government regulation.

Between 8 and 14 weeks of age, use every opportunity to expose the pup to as many people and situations as possible. This is part of the critical socialization period that will determine how good a pet your dog will become. This is not the time to abandon a puppy for eight hours while you go to work. This is also not the time to punish your dog in any way, shape or form.

This is the time to introduce your dog to neighborhood cats, birds and other creatures. Hold off on exposure to other dogs until after the second vaccination in the series. You don't want your new friend to pick up contagious diseases from dogs it meets in its travels before it has adequate protection. By 12 weeks of age, your pup should be ready for social outings with other dogs. Go on them—they're a great way for your dog to feel comfortable around members of its own species. Walk the streets and introduce your pup to everybody you meet. Your goal should be to introduce your dog to every type of person or situation it is likely to encounter in its life. Take it in cars, elevators, buses, travel crates, subways, parade grounds, beaches—you want it to habituate to all environments. Expose your pup to kids, teenagers, old people, people in wheelchairs, people on bicycles and people in uniforms. The more varied the exposure, the better the socialization.

Proper identification of your pet is also important since this minimizes the risk of theft and increases the chances that your pet will be returned to you if it is lost. There are several different options. Microchip implantation is a relatively painless procedure involving the subcutaneous injection of an implant the size of a grain of rice. This implant does not act as a beacon if your pet goes missing. However, if your pet turns up at a veterinary clinic or shelter and is checked with a scanner, the chip provides information about the owner that can be used to quickly reunite you with your pet. This method of identification is reasonably priced, permanent in nature, and performed at most veterinary clinics. Another option is tattooing, which can be done on the inner ear or on the skin of the abdomen. Most purebreds are given a number by the associated registry (e.g., American Kennel Club, United Kennel Club, Canadian Kennel Club, etc.) and this is used for identification. Alternatively, permanent numbers such as social security numbers (telephone numbers and addresses may change during the life of your pet) can be used in the tattooing process. There are several different tattoo registries maintaining lists of dogs, their tattoo codes and their owners. Finally, identifying collars and tags provide quick information but can be separated from your pet if it is lost of stolen. They work best when combined with a permanent identification system such as microchip implantation or tattooing.

FOUR TO SIX MONTHS OF AGE

At 16 weeks of age, when your pup gets the last in its series of regular induction vaccinations, ask your veterinarian about evaluating the pup for hip dysplasia with the PennHip™ technique. This helps predict the risk of developing hip dysplasia as well as degenerative joint disease. Cocker Spaniel breeders have done an excellent job decreasing the incidence of hip dysplasia through routine screening and registration programs. Since anesthesia is typically required for the procedure, many veterinarians like to do the evaluation at the same time as neutering.

At this same time, it is very worthwhile to perform a diagnostic test for von Willebrand's disease, an inherited disorder that causes uncontrolled bleeding. This trait is fairly common in the Cocker Spaniel. The breed also has a high incidence of two other bleeding disorders, Hemophilia B and Factor X Deficiency, and these can all be tested at the same time. An additional test worth considering is one that can screen for phosphofructokinase deficiency. A simple blood test is all that is required, but it may need to be sent to a special laboratory to have the test performed. You will be extremely happy you had the foresight to have this done before neutering. If your dog does have a bleeding problem, it will be necessary to take special precautions during surgery.

As a general rule, neuter your animal at about six months of age unless you fully intend to

If you stick to the schedule your veterinarian suggests for regular check-ups and you start out with a sound pup, your dog will be the picture of good health.

breed it. As mentioned earlier, neutering can be safely done at eight weeks of age, but this is still not a common practice. Neutering not only stops the possibility of pregnancy and undesirable behaviors, but can prevent several health problems as well. It is a well established fact that pups spayed before their first heat have a dramatically reduced incidence of mammary (breast) cancer. Neutered males significantly decrease their incidence of prostate disorders.

Also when your pet is six months of age, your veterinarian will want to take a blood sample to perform a heartworm test. If the test is negative and shows no evidence of heartworm infection, the pup

will go on heartworm prevention therapy. Some veterinarians are even recommending preventive therapy in younger pups. This might be a one-a-day regimen, but newer therapies can be given on a once-a-month basis. As a bonus, most of these heartworm preventatives also help prevent internal parasites (worms, as mentioned above).

If your Cocker Spaniel has any patches of hair loss, your veterinarian will want to perform a skin scraping with a scalpel blade to see if any *Demodex* mites are responsible. If there is a problem, don't lose hope; about 90 percent of demodicosis cases can be cured with supportive care only.

However, it's important to diagnose it early before scarring results.

Another part of the six-month visit should be a thorough dental evaluation to make sure all the permanent teeth have correctly erupted. If they haven't, this will be the time to correct the problem. Correction should only be performed to make the animal more comfortable and promote more normal chewing. The procedures should never be used to cosmetically improve the appearance of a dog used for show purposes or breeding.

After the dental evaluation, you should start implementing home dental care. In most cases, this will consist of brushing the teeth one or more times each week and perhaps using dental rinses. It is a sad fact that 85 percent of dogs over four years

A thorough dental evaluation can be done at six months of age.

of age have periodontal disease and doggy breath. In fact it is so common that most people think it is "normal." Well, it is normal- as normal as bad breath would be in people if they never brushed their teeth. Brush your dog's teeth regularly with a special tooth brush and toothpaste and you can greatly reduce the incidence of tartar buildup, bad breath and gum disease. Better preventive care means that dogs live a long time. They'll enjoy their sunset years more if they still have their teeth. Ask your veterinarian for details on home dental care.

ONE TO SEVEN YEARS OF AGE

At one year of age, your dog should be re-examined again and have boosters for all vaccines. Your veterinarian will also want to do a very thorough physical examination to look for early evidence of problems. This might include taking radiographs (x-rays) of the hips and elbows to look for evidence of dysplastic changes. Genetic Disease Control (GDC) will certify hips and elbows at 12 months of age; Orthopedic Foundation for Animals won't issue certification until 24 months of age.

At 12 months of age, it's also a great time to have some blood

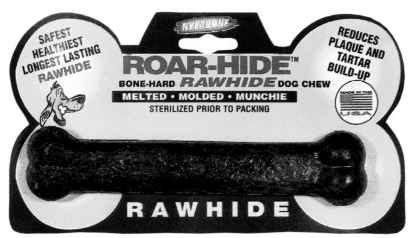

Keep a supply of chew toys on hand to promote dental health. The Roarhide® is a tasty chew for any dog.

samples analyzed to provide background information. Although few Cockers experience clinical problems at this young age, troubles may be starting. Therefore, it is a good idea to have baseline levels of thyroid hormones (free and total), TSH (Thyroid-stimulating hormone), blood cell counts, organ chemistries, and cholesterol levels. This can serve as a valuable comparison to samples collected in the future. It may also help identify those Cockers that develop liver disease (hepatitis) due to copper accumulation.

Each year, preferably around the time of your pet's birthday, it's time for another veterinary visit. This visit is a wonderful opportunity for a thorough clinical examination rather than just

"shots." Since 85 percent of dogs have periodontal disease by four years of age, veterinary intervention does not seem to be as widespread as it should be. The examination should include visually inspecting the ears, eyes (a great time to start scrutinizing for progressive retinal atrophy, cataracts, etc.), mouth (don't wait for gum disease), and groin, listening (auscultation) to the lungs and heart, feeling (palpating) the lymph nodes and abdomen, and answering all of your questions about optimal health care. In addition, booster vaccinations are given during these times, feces are checked for parasites, urine is analyzed and blood samples may be collected for analysis. One of the tests run on the blood sample is for heartworm antigen. In areas of the country where heartworm is only present in the spring, summer and fall (it's spread by mosquitoes), blood samples are collected and evaluated about a month prior to the mosquito season. Other routine blood tests are for blood cells (hematology), organ chemistries, thyroid levels and electrolytes.

By two years of age, most veterinarians prefer to begin preventive dental cleanings, often referred to as "prophies." Anesthesia is required and the veterinarian or veterinary dentist will use an ultrasonic scaler to remove plaque and tartar from above and below the gum line and polish the teeth so that plaque has a harder time sticking to the teeth. Radiographs (x-rays) and fluoride treatments are other options. It is now known that it is plaque, not tartar, that initiates inflammation in the gums. Since scaling and root planing remove more tartar than plaque, veterinary dentists have begun using a new technique called PerioBUD (Periodontal Bactericidal Ultrasonic Debridement). The ultrasonic treatment is quicker, disrupts more bacteria and is less irritating to the gums. With tooth polishing to finish up the procedure, gum healing is better and

Veterinarians like to give dogs regular dental cleanings, during which they scale off plaque and tartar.

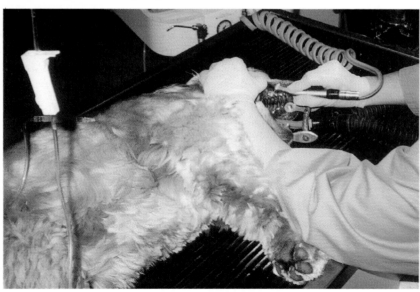

These three Cockers have healthy coats in the colors of black, buff and brown-and-tan.

owners can start home care sooner. Each dog has its own dental needs that must be addressed, but most veterinary dentists recommend prophies annually.

At four to five years of age, your veterinarian will probably want to start screening for dilated cardiomyopathy, since this is so common in Cocker Spaniels. Chest radiographs (x-rays) aren't usually too helpful; ultrasound examinations (echocardiography) and electrocardiograms (EKGs) are the preferred tests. Annual tests are usually sufficient and it is extremely important to diagnose the condition early because it is such a devastating and life-threatening disease.

SENIOR COCKER SPANIELS

Cocker Spaniels are considered seniors when they reach about seven years of age. Veterinarians still usually only need to examine them once a year, but it is now important to start screening for geriatric problems. Accordingly blood profiles, urinalysis, chest radiographs (x-rays) and electrocardiograms (EKG) are recommended on an annual basis. When problems are caught early, they are much more likely to be successfully managed. This is as true in canine medicine as it is in human medicine.

MEDICAL PROBLEMS

**RECOGNIZED GENETIC CONDITIONS SPECIFICALLY
RELATED TO THE COCKER SPANIEL**

Many conditions appear to be especially prominent in Cocker Spaniels. Sometimes it is possible to identify the genetic basis of a problem, but in many cases, we must be satisfied with merely identifying the breeds that are at risk and how the conditions can be identified, treated and prevented.

Facing page: If you know your Cocker is prone to a particular problem, you can watch or test for it as he grows.

Following are some conditions that have been recognized as being common in the Cocker Spaniel, but this listing is certainly not complete. Also, many genetic conditions may be common in certain breed lines, not in the breed in general.

BLEEDING DISORDERS

Cocker Spaniels are prone to several different bleeding disorders, including von Willebrand's disease, Factor IX deficiency (Hemophilia B) and Factor X deficiency. Hemophilia B is a sex-linked recessive trait, meaning the females carry the trait but males are most often affected. Factor X deficiency is autosomal incompletely dominant, meaning that only one parent need carry the trait for pups to be affected. Both of these can result in bruising and prolonged bleeding. In some cases, Hemophilia B can result in life-threatening hemorrhage. The diagnosis can be confirmed by performing clotting profiles. The best routine screening procedure involves an activated partial thromboplastin time (or Activated Clotting Time) and Prothrombin time (PT). The Prothrombin time will be abnormal for Factor X deficiency but normal for Hemophilia B while the Partial Thromboplastin Time (and Activated Clotting Time) will be severely prolonged for Hemophilia B and moderately prolonged for Factor X deficiency. Specific tests can be performed for these factors if your veterinarian feels they are warranted. Treatment is supportive when animals have bleeding episodes and there are no cures. For affected animals it is best to reduce risk by avoiding elective surgery, rough play, internal/external parasites and medications that may affect clotting (such as aspirin). For those with Hemophilia B, the dam should be considered a definite carrier and not used for future breedings. For those with Factor X deficiency, parents should be tested for carrier status and the appropriate individual should be removed from breeding programs.

CATARACTS

Cataracts refer to an opacity or cloudiness on the lens, and ophthalmologists are careful to categorize them on the basis of stage, age of onset, and location. In Cocker Spaniels, cataracts are inherited as an autosomal recessive trait, meaning that both parents need carry the trait for pups to be affected. The cataracts may be juvenile or adult in onset and are described as being cortical and progressive. Many dogs adapt well to cataracts, but cataract removal surgery is available and quite successful if needed. The condition may be associated with persistent hyperplastic primary vitreous as discussed below. Affected animals, their siblings and parents should obviously not be used for breeding and careful ophthalmologic evaluation of both parents is warranted.

DILATED CARDIOMYOPATHY

Dilated cardiomyopathy refers to a defect of the heart muscle in which the heart muscle becomes thin and stretched, much like a balloon. In that condition, it is not a very effective pump and, eventually, affected dogs die from heart failure. Cocker Spaniels are one of the most commonly affected breeds; this is an extremely important and deadly problem in the breed.

Although a genetic tendency is suspected, long-term studies are not yet available. Recent studies in the Cocker Spaniel seem to suggest that taurine (an amino acid) may be implicated, as it is in the feline form of the disease. As if this isn't confusing enough, some researchers suspect that viruses might also be involved since there is some human research indicating that this might be the case in people.

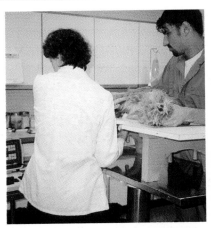

Radiologist Dr. Marcia Whiteley performs an echocardiogram to rule out cardiomyopathy.

Early in the course of the disease, affected animals seem normal. It is only when they show signs of heart failure that most owners seek veterinary attention. Early signs might include depression, coughing, exercise intolerance, weakness, respiratory distress, decreased appetite, and even fainting. Thus, routine thorough veterinary examinations are very important, especially in the young and middle-aged adult.

In some cases the heart rate is increased, and this might indicate atrial fibrillation, a common sequel to cardiomyopathy. However, in most cases, radiographs (x-rays), electrocardiograms (EKGs) and echocardiograms (ultrasound examinations) are required for definitive diagnosis. Echocardiograms are painless studies using ultrasound examination that are extremely useful in making the diagnosis. Electrocardiograms (EKGs) also have their place. Recent studies have shown that most dogs with early cardiomyopathy have ventricular premature contractions (VPCs), which are indicators of increased risk to developing actual cardiomyopathy. These VPCs may not be evident all the time when EKGs are taken, so 24-hour studies with a Holter monitor are sometimes necessary, as they are in people.

There is no cure for cardiomyopathy, but some breeds respond well to megadoses of specific nutrients. In the Cocker Spaniel, this means taurine at 500 milligrams twice daily. Veterinary formulations are available as well as over-the-counter supplements from health supply shops. Coenzyme Q may also be beneficial and is available in non-prescription form. For those cases that don't respond to nutritional supplementation, digoxin (a digitalis derivative) is often used to treat the condition, as are beta-1 blockers and vasodilators. Milrinone, an experimental drug, has been very effective in dogs with heart muscle failure but is not yet available for dogs

or people. All dogs with cardiomyopathy that are treated with drugs only eventually succumb to their disease.

Right now there are no foolproof ways to prevent cardiomyopathy. The best choice is to avoid pups that have a family history of cardiomyopathy. In many cases it will be necessary to know medical history back at least three generations. Several researchers are trying to determine the genetic link for cardiomyopathy using DNA testing. If that is successful, it may be possible to prevent the condition by selecting unaffected breeding partners based on tissue testing.

ELBOW DYSPLASIA

Elbow dysplasia doesn't refer to just one disease, but rather an entire complex of disorders that affect the elbow joint. Several different processes might be involved, including ununited anconeal process, fragmented medial coronoid process, osteochondritis of the medial humeral condyle or incomplete ossification of the humeral condyle. Incomplete ossification of the humeral condyle is relatively rare but achieves importance because the condition is almost unique to the Cocker Spaniel. Elbow dysplasia is a dis-

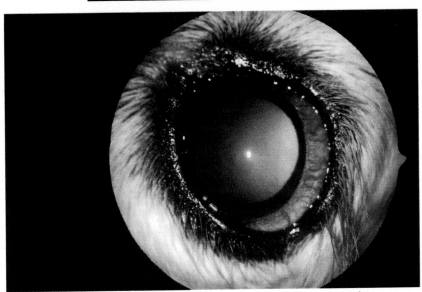

A dog with acute glaucoma being examined under the microscope.

order of young dogs, with problems usually starting between four and seven months of age. The usual manifestation is a sudden onset of lameness. In time, the continued inflammation results in arthritis in those affected joints.

Radiographs (x-rays) are taken of the elbow joints and submitted to a registry for evaluation. The Orthopedic Foundation for Animals (OFA) will assign a breed registry number to those animals with normal elbows that are over 24 months of age. Abnormal elbows are reported as Grade I to III, where Grade III elbows have well-developed degenerative joint disease (arthritis). Normal elbows

on individuals 24 months or older are assigned a breed registry number and are periodically reported to parent breed clubs. Genetic Disease Control for Animals (GDC) maintains an open registry for elbow dysplasia and assigns a registry number to those individuals with normal elbows at one to two months of age or older. Only animals with "normal" elbows should be used for breeding.

GLAUCOMA

Glaucoma is one of the leading causes of blindness in animals and is caused by an increase in fluid pressure within the eye. Anything that interferes with the drainage of fluid inside the eye can result in glaucoma, and not all have a genetic basis. However, primary glaucoma does occur in several breeds, including the Cocker Spaniel. There are three distinct types of inherited glaucoma: narrow-angle (as seen in Cocker Spaniels); open-angle (as seen in Beagles), and; goniodysgenesis (as seen in Cocker Spaniels). Thus, Cockers are susceptible to two different forms of glaucoma.

With glaucoma, the eyes are often red and painful. Most Cocker Spaniels are over three years of age when first affected. The diagnosis is confirmed with a tonometer that measures the

This radiograph displays a dog that received an OFA "excellent" when x-rayed for hip dysplasia. Both of the hip joints are clear.

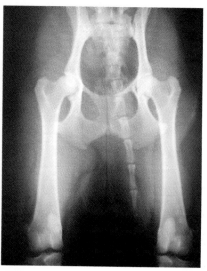

pressure within the eye. Gonioscopy is a technique used to visually inspect the drainage angle within the eye and determine the exact cause of the problem. Treatment can involve medical or surgical options depending on the severity of the disorder. Hereditary glaucoma can be prevented by screening all animals used in breeding programs.

HIP DYSPLASIA

Hip dysplasia is a genetically transmitted developmental problem of the hip joint that is common in many breeds. Dogs may be born with a "susceptibility" or "tendency" to develop hip dysplasia, but it is not a foregone conclusion that all susceptible dogs will eventually develop hip dysplasia. All dysplastic dogs are born with normal hips and the dysplastic changes begin within the first 24 months of life although they are usually evident long before then.

It is now known that there are several factors that help determine whether a susceptible dog will ever develop hip dysplasia. These include body size, conformation, growth patterns, caloric load and electrolyte balance in the dog food.

Although Cocker Spaniels are often cited as being prone to hip dysplasia, based on research tabulated up to January, 1995, the Orthopedic Foundation for Animals concluded that 7.5 percent of the radiographs submitted from Cocker Spaniels had evidence of hip dysplasia. This is great news because the Cocker Spaniel breeders have been able to reduce the incidence in the breed by 40-50 percent just through conscientious breeding.

When purchasing a Cocker Spaniel pup, it is best to ensure that the parents were both registered with normal hips through one of the international registries, such as the Orthopedic Foundation for Animals or Genetic Disease Control. Pups over 16 weeks of age can be tested by veterinarians trained in the PennHip™ procedure, which is a way of predicting risk of developing hip dysplasia and arthritis. In time it should be possible to completely eradicate hip dysplasia from the breed.

If you start with a pup with less risk of hip dysplasia you can further reduce your risk by controlling its environment. Select a food with a moderate amount of protein and avoid the super-high premium and high-calorie diets. Also, feed your pup several times a day for defined periods (e.g., 15 minutes) rather than leaving the food down all day. Avoid all nutritional supplements, especially those that include calcium, phosphorus and/or vitamin D. Use controlled exercise for your pup rather than letting him run loose. Unrestricted exercise in the pup can stress the joints, which are still developing.

If you have a dog with hip dysplasia, all is not lost. There is much variability in the clinical presentation. Some dogs with severe dysplasia experience little pain while others that have minor changes may be extremely sore. The main problem is that dysplastic hips promote degenerative joint disease (osteoarthritis or osteoarthrosis), which can eventually incapacitate the joint. Aspirin and other anti-inflammatory agents are suitable in the early stages; surgery is needed when animals are in great pain, when drug therapy doesn't work adequately, or when movement is severely compromised.

HYPOTHYROIDISM

Hypothyroidism is the most commonly diagnosed endocrine (hormonal) problem in the Cocker Spaniel. The disease itself refers to an insufficient amount of thyroid hormones being produced. Although there are several different potential causes, lymphocytic thyroiditis is by far the most common. Iodine deficiency and goiter are extremely rare. In lymphocytic thyroiditis, the body produces antibodies that target aspects of thyroid tissue; the process usually starts between one and three years of age in affected animals but doesn't become clinically evident until later in life.

There is a great deal of misinformation about hypothyroidism. Owners often expect their dog to be obese with the condition and otherwise don't suspect it. The fact is that hypothyroidism is quite variable in its manifestations and obesity is only seen in a small percentage of cases. In most cases, affected animals appear fine until they use up most of their remaining thyroid hormone reserves. The most common manifestations then are lack of energy and recurrent infections. Hair loss is seen in about one-third of cases.

You might suspect that hypothyroidism would be easy to diagnose but it is trickier than you think. Since there is a large reserve of thyroid hormones in the body, a test measuring only total blood levels of the hormones (T-4 and T-3) is not a very sensitive indicator of the condition. Thyroid stimulation tests are the best way to measure the functional reserve. Measuring "free" and "total" levels of the hormones or endogenous TSH (thyroid-stimulating hormone) are other approaches. Also, since we know that most cases are due to antibodies produced in the body, screening for these autoantibodies can help identify animals at risk of developing hypothyroidism.

Obesity is only occasionally associated with hypothyroidism.

Because this breed is so prone to developing hypothyroidism, periodic "screening" for the disorder is warranted in many cases. Although none of the screening tests is perfect, a basic panel evaluating total T-4, free T-4, TSH and cholesterol levels is a good start. Ideally, this would first be performed at one year of age and annually thereafter. This "screening" is practical, because none of these tests are very expensive.

Fortunately, although there may be some problems in diagnosing hypothyroidism, treatment is straightforward and relatively inexpensive. Supplementing the affected animal twice daily with thyroid hormone effectively treats the condition. In many breeds, supplementation with thyroid hormones is commonly done to help confirm the diagnosis. However, since thyroid hormones affect the heart, and since Cocker Spaniels are so prone to the heart disease cardiomyopathy, thyroid hormone supplementation should be reserved for those animals with well-documented hypothyroidism. Animals with hypothyroidism should not be used in a breeding program, and those with circulating autoantibodies but no actual hypothyroid disease should also not be used for breeding.

INCOMPLETE OSSIFICATION OF HUMERAL CONDYLE

Over the past decade, fractures of the humeral condyles of the elbow joint have been recognized to occur disproportionately in spaniels, especially Cocker Spaniels. In one published study of 28 affected dogs, 24 were Cocker Spaniels, 3 were Brittany Spaniels and the last was a Cocker Spaniel-Standard Poodle cross. The cause is unknown but it is hypothesized that there is a genetic basis for the condition. Genetic evaluation is being conducted at North Carolina State University, College of Veterinary Medicine.

Typically, the cartilage in this area turns to bone (ossifies) by 8-12 weeks of age. This ossification fails to occur completely in affected spaniels. This causes the bone to be weakened, and affected dogs may suffer from spontaneous fractures following even minor trauma. Most are adults (2 to 12 years of age, average 6 years of age) when they experience problems, and the majority so far have been males. Because these dogs are older, most veterinarians in clinical practice haven't considered a hereditary nature. However, given the facts to date, incomplete ossification of the humeral condyle should be considered in any adult spaniel experiencing front leg lameness. Diagnosis of the condylar fracture is not difficult with radiographs (x-rays), but identifying affected individuals before the fracture occurs is more difficult. High-resolution radiographs may identify a fault in the condyles (always evaluate both front legs!) but this is more accurately determined by computed tomography (CAT scans), which is an impractical tool for routine screening. The fractures themselves require surgical correction. Transcondylar bone screws are recommended because of the weakness of the condyles for regular fixation methods. Because of the likely genetic nature of this problem, affected animals, their parents and siblings should not be used for breeding.

LIVER DISEASE DUE TO COPPER ACCUMULATION

Some dogs are prone to developing liver disease in association with an inherited metabolic defect which causes copper to accumulate in the liver and lead to toxicity. This is similar to Wilson's Disease in people. The Cocker Spaniel is not the breed affected most often (that would be the Bedlington Terrier), but the incidence is high enough to warrant mention here. The con-

dition is spread as a recessive trait so both parents must be carriers if a dog is found to be affected.

Affected dogs develop a slowly progressive form of liver disease. They are usually in young adulthood when the condition is first recognized. Jaundice only develops late in the course of the disease when liver function is severely compromised.

Very recently, researchers have discovered a genetic marker for copper toxicosis that can be detected by a blood test. Although not yet widely available as a commercial test, this laboratory evaluation is an exceptionally important method for detecting carriers of the disease. Those carriers should be removed from all breeding possibilities and then it should be possible to completely eliminate the trait in Cocker Spaniels.

MEDIAL PATELLAR LUXATION

The patella is the kneecap and patellar luxation refers to the condition when the kneecap slips out of its usual resting place and lodges on the inside (medial aspect) of the knee. It is a congenital problem of dogs, but the degree of patellar displacement may increase with time as the tissues stretch and the bones continue to deform. The condition is seen primarily in small and toy breeds of dogs.

Medial patellar luxation may be graded by veterinarians as to how much laxity there is in the patella. No laxity is preferred and affected individuals may have Grade 1 (mild) through Grade IV (severe). The diagnosis can be made by manipulating the knee joint to see if the kneecap luxates towards the inner (medial) aspect of the leg. There is usually little or no pain associated with this process. Radiography (x-rays) can be used to document persistent luxation and to evaluate for other abnormalities such as arthritic changes.

Older dogs and those mildly affected may respond to conservative therapy, but surgery is often recommended for young dogs before arthritic changes become evident. There are several successful surgical techniques for this condition. After surgery, dogs should have enforced rest for six weeks while healing, and leash activity only. The results are excellent in most cases.

The best form of prevention is to only purchase animals that have no family history of medial patellar luxation. Registries are maintained by the Orthopedic Foundation for Animals (OFA) and the Institute for Genetic Disease Control in Animals (GDC).

NARCOLEPSY

Narcolepsy is a sleep disorder in which animals may spontaneously fall asleep without association to tiredness. Affected pups usually start to have problems between 4 and 20 weeks of age; they often have more attacks as they get excited or try to eat or sleep. The condition can be conclusively diagnosed based on food-elicited cataplexy testing should that prove necessary. Various drugs such as yohimbine and imipramine have been used in treatment, but many Cockers tend to have fewer attacks as they get older.

The condition can be prevented if relatives of affected pups are not used in breeding. This includes normal siblings, parents and their siblings and grandparents and their siblings. Hopefully we'll have a predictive test one day so that potential breeding pairs can be screened, but that is not an option at present.

PATENT DUCTUS ARTERIOSUS

Patent ductus arteriosus (PDA) is the most common congenital heart defect seen in dogs.

This is inherited as a polygenic threshold trait, meaning that the trait is controlled by a number of different genes and has a threshold since, clinically, there can only be a hole (patency) or no hole, no clinical intermediate. This defect occurs when the normal fetal communication between the nonfunctional lungs and the aorta (major blood vessel leaving the heart) fails after birth. This results in the shunting of blood into the pulmonary artery (major vessel to the lungs) and flooding of the lungs. At the same time the rest of the body is getting an inadequate amount of circulation.

Most puppies with PDA show no clinical signs early in life, but a heart murmur is detected upon examination for first vaccination. Other puppies may develop acute heart failure and have difficulty in breathing, exercise intolerance, or develop a cough.

An example of prolapsed third eyelid glands in both eyes.

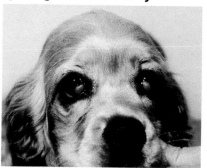

The diagnosis of PDA is normally made by the characteristic murmur, electrocardiogram (EKG) and chest radiographs (X-rays). Surgery is needed to correct the condition. The surgery should be done as soon as possible, ideally before five months of age to minimize secondary damage to the heart and lungs. There is over a 90 percent success rate with the surgery and, if completed early enough, the prognosis is excellent that the dog will be able to live a normal life expectancy. If left uncorrected, the puppies usually do not live more than the first year or two.

PROGRESSIVE RETINAL ATROPHY

Progressive retinal atrophy (PRA) refers to several inherited disorders affecting the retina that result in blindness. PRA is thought to be inherited, with each breed demonstrating a specific age of onset and pattern of inheritance. In the Cocker Spaniel, there is a late onset of problems and the disease gene has been characterized as *prcd*. This represents a mutation in the same allelic gene. The condition is transmitted genetically as an autosomal recessive trait, meaning that both parents must be carriers.

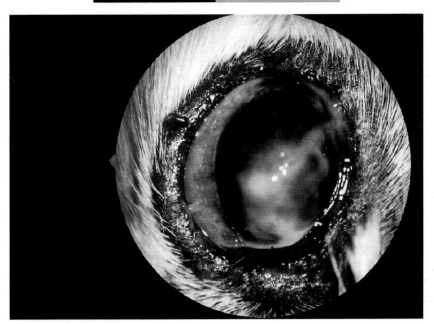

Keratoconjunctivitis sicca (KCS) is more familiarly known as "dry eye". It is pictured here under a microscope.

There is progressive atrophy or degeneration of the retinal tissue. Visual impairment occurs slowly but progressively. Therefore, animals often adapt to their reduced vision until it is compromised to near blindness. Because of this, owners may not notice any visual impairment until the condition has progressed significantly.

Retinal degeneration implies that the retina was normal at birth and later developed problems. This is the subtype of PRA seen in the Cocker Spaniel. Because dogs have many other well-developed senses, such as smell and hearing, their lack of sight is usually not immediately evident. The loss of vision is slow but progressive, and blindness eventually results.

The diagnosis of PRA can be made in two ways: direct visualization of the retina, and electroretinography (ERG). The use of indirect ophthalmoscopy requires a great deal of training and expertise and is more commonly performed by ophthalmology specialists than general practitioners. Diagnostic changes are not usually apparent until three to five years of age. An additional highly sensitive test, usually available only from specialists, is "electroretinography" or ERG. The procedure is painless, but usually available only from specialty centers. This instrument is sensitive enough to detect even the early onset of disease. In the Cocker Spaniel, diagnostic changes are usually evident by nine months of age.

Unfortunately there is no treatment available for progressive retinal atrophy, and all affected dogs eventually go blind. Identification of affected breeding animals is essential to prevent spread of the condition within the breed. Breeding animals should be examined annually by a veterinary ophthalmologist. A DNA test for PRA-affected and carrier animals has been formulated for use in Irish Setters and can be conducted on a single blood test. Future research is necessary to create a suitable test for the form of progressive rod-cone degeneration seen in the Cocker Spaniel.

SEBORRHEA

Seborrhea is a primary defect in the skin's ability to replenish its supply of cells. Although the term seborrhea is loosely used for any greasy skin condition, Cocker Spaniels are prone to the primary inherited form of the disease. Most other cases that are referred to loosely as seborrhea are actually secondary to an underlying disease process, such as an allergy or hypothyroidism. Research to date has shown that the epidermal cells of affected animals have a greatly accelerated turnover rate, which causes them to

This photo shows the effect of tearing from atresia of the puncta (closed tear ducts). Notice the brown stain below the eye.

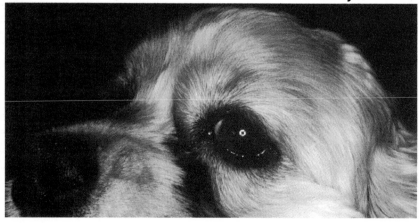

You can run—but you can't hide—from medical problems, which is why it's best to have a veterinarian you know and trust.

collect in a haphazard fashion on the skin surface. The defect has been identified and is located in the skin itself. Thus, if a sample of affected skin was grafted onto a normal animal, the problem would persist in that defined area. Similarly, skin taken from a normal animal and grafted onto one with seborrhea would maintain skin normalcy in that particular area.

The result is an animal that is born normal but by early adulthood has started to develop greasy skin, a disagreeable odor and inflammation on the skin surface. The ears also often develop a waxy discharge. In time, there is thickened skin, loss of fur and variable itchiness. Secondary bacterial and yeast infections are commonplace. Treatment is symptomatic and there are currently no cures. Frequent shampooing with antiseborrheic products (e.g., benzoyl peroxide, tar, selenium disulfide) is necessary. Some animals respond well to vitamin A derivatives (retinoids) such as etretinate. Affected animals should definitely not be used for breeding.

VON WILLEBRAND'S DISEASE

Von Willebrand's disease (vWD) is the most common inherited bleeding disorder of dogs. The abnormal gene can be inherited from one or both parents. If both parents pass on the gene, most of the resultant pups fail to thrive and most will die. In most cases, though, the pup inherits a relative lack of clotting ability, which is quite variable. For instance, one dog may have 15 percent of the clotting factor, while another might have 60 percent. The higher the amount, the less likely it will be that the bleeding will be readily evident since spontaneous bleeding is usually only seen when dogs have less than 30 percent of the normal level of von Willebrand clotting factor. Thus, some dogs don't get diagnosed until they are neutered or spayed, and they end up bleeding uncontrollably or they develop pockets of blood (hematomas) at the surgical site. In addition to the inherited form of vWD, this disorder can also be acquired in association with familial hypothyroidism. This form is usually seen in Cocker Spaniels older than five years of age.

Von Willebrand's disease is extremely important in the Cocker Spaniel because the incidence appears to be on the rise. However, there is good news. There are tests available to determine the amount of von Willebrand factor in the blood, and they are accurate and reasonably priced. Cockers used for breeding should have normal amounts of von Willebrand factor in their blood and so should all pups that are adopted as household pets. Carriers should not be used for breeding, even if they appear clinically normal. Since hypothyroidism can be linked with von Willebrand's disease, thyroid profiles can also be a useful part of the screening procedure in older Cocker Spaniels.

Von Willebrand's disease, a bleeding disorder, appears to be on the rise in Cocker Spaniels.

OTHER CONDITIONS SEEN IN THE COCKER SPANIEL

- Atrioventricular Block
- Basal-cell Tumor
- Cerebellar Abiotrophy
- Ceroid Lipofuscinosis
- Cleft Palate
- Congenital Hypotrichosis
- Congenital Vestibular Disease
- Corneal Dystrophy
- Cranioschisis
- Cryptorchidism
- Cyclic Hematopoiesis
- Diaphragmatic Hernia
- Distichiasis
- Ectopic Cilia
- Ectropion
- Ectropion/Entropion
- Encircling Third Eyelid
- Entropion
- Esophageal Motility Disorders
- Harelip
- Hermaphrodism
- Hydrocephalus
- Imperforate Lacrimal Puncta
- Inguinal Hernia
- Keratoconjunctivitis Sicca
- Lens Subluxation
- Lip fold dermatitis
- Malocclusion

- Melanoma
- Microphakia
- Myotonia
- Obesity
- Optic Nerve Colobomas
- Optic Nerve Hypoplasia
- Oversized Palpebral Fissure
- Pelger-Huet Anomaly
- Persistent Pupillary Membranes
- Phosphofructokinase (PFK) Deficiency
- Posterior Polymorphous Dystrophy
- Prolapse of Third Eyelid Gland
- Proliferative Episcleritis
- Redundant Forehead Skin
- Renal Cortical Hypoplasia
- Retinal Dysplasia
- Trichomegaly
- Tubulointerstitial fibrosis
- Umbilical Hernia
- Urolithiasis
- Valvular Insufficiency
- Vitamin A-responsive Dermatosis
- XX Male Syndrome

INFECTIONS &
INFESTATIONS

**HOW TO PROTECT YOUR COCKER SPANIEL
FROM PARASITES AND MICROBES**

An important part of keeping your Cocker Spaniel healthy is to prevent problems caused by parasites and microbes. Although there are a variety of drugs available that can help limit problems, prevention is always the desired option.

Facing page: Whenever you've spent time outside with your Cocker, check him for parasites like ticks.

FLEAS

Fleas are important and common parasites, but not an inevitable part of every pet owner's reality. If you take the time to understand some of the basics of flea population dynamics, control is both conceivable and practical.

Fleas have four life stages (egg, larva, pupa, adult), and each stage responds to some therapies while being resistant to others. Failing to understand this is the major reason why some people have so much trouble getting the upper hand in the battle to control fleas.

Fleas spend all their time on dogs and only leave if physically removed by brushing, bathing or scratching. However, the eggs that are laid on the animal are not sticky and fall to the ground to contaminate the environment. Our goal must be to remove fleas from the animals in the house, from the house itself and from the immediate outdoor environment. Part of our plan must also involve using different medications to get rid of the different life stages, as well as minimizing the use of potentially harmful insecticides that could be poisonous for pets and family members.

A flea comb is a very handy device for recovering fleas from pets. The best places to comb are the top of the tail, groin area, armpits, back and neck region. Fleas collected should be dropped into a container of alcohol, which quickly kills them before they can escape. In addition, all pets should be bathed with a cleansing shampoo (or flea shampoo) to remove fleas and eggs. This has no residual effect, however, and fleas can jump back on immediately after the bath if nothing else is done. Rather than using potent insecticidal dips and sprays, consider products containing the safe pyrethrins, imidacloprid or fipronil and the insect growth regulators (such as methoprene and pyripoxyfen) or insect development inhibitors (IDIs) such as iufenuron. These products are not only extremely safe, but the combination is effective against eggs, larvae and adults. This only leaves the pupal stage to cause continued problems. insect growth regulators can also be

The cat flea is the most comon flea of both dogs and cats. Courtesy of Fleabusters, Rx for Fleas, Inc.

safely given as once-a-month oral preparations. Flea collars are rarely useful, and electronic flea collars are not to be recommended for any dogs.

To clean up the household, vacuuming is a good first step because it picks up about 50 percent of the flea eggs and it also stimulates flea pupae to emerge as adults, a stage when they are easier to kill with insecticides. The vacuum bag should then be removed and discarded with each treatment. Household treatment can then be initiated with pyrethrins and a combination of either insect growth regulators or sodium polyborate (a borax derivative). The pyrethrins need to be reapplied every two to three weeks, but the insect growth regulators last about two to three months and many companies guarantee sodium polyborate for a full year. Stronger insecticides such as carbamates and organophosphates can be used and will last three to four weeks in the household, but they are potentially toxic and offer no real advantages other than their persistence in the home environment. This is also one of their major disadvantages.

When an insecticide is combined with an insect growth regulator, flea control is most likely

Getting rid of the fleas on your dog is just part of alleviating a flea problem. You will need to treat your home and yard, as well.

to be successful. The insecticide kills the adult fleas and the insect growth regulator affects the eggs and larvae. However, insecticides kill less that 20 percent of flea cocoons (pupae). Because of this, new fleas may hatch in two to three weeks despite appropriate application of products. This is known as the "pupal window," and is one of the most common causes for ineffective flea control. This is why a safe insecticide should be applied to the home environment two to three weeks after the initial treatment. This catches the newly-hatched pupae before they have a chance to lay eggs and continue the flea problem.

If treatment of the outdoor environment is needed, there are several options. Pyripoxyfen, an insect growth regulator, is

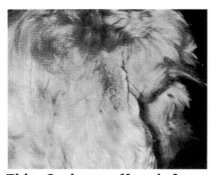

This Cocker suffered from moderate itching for years due to allergies. When the itching became more severe, skin scrapings revealed sarcoptic mange.

The Cocker's allergic itching continued. Note the redness and inflammation involving the chest, abdomen and elbows.

stable in sunlight and can be used outdoors. Sodium polyborate can be used as well, but it is important that it not be inadvertently eaten by pets. Organophosphates and carbamates are sometimes recommended for outdoor use and it is not necessary to treat the entire property. Flea control should be directed predominantly at garden margins, porches, dog houses, garages, and in other pet lounging areas. Fleas don't do well with direct exposure to sunlight, so generalized lawn treatment is not needed. Finally, microscopic worms (nematodes) are available that can be sprayed onto the lawn with a garden sprayer. The nematodes eat immature flea forms and then biodegrade without harming anything else.

TICKS

Ticks are found worldwide and can cause a variety of problems including blood loss, tick paralysis, Lyme disease, "tick fever," Rocky Mountain Spotted Fever and babesiosis. All are important diseases which need to be prevented whenever possible. This is only possible by limiting the exposure of our pets to ticks.

For those species of tick that dwell indoors, the eggs are laid mostly in cracks and on vertical surfaces in kennels and homes. Otherwise, most other species are found outside in vegetation, such as grassy meadows, woods, brush, and weeds.

Ticks feed only on blood but they don't actually bite. They attach to an animal by sticking their harpoon-shaped mouthparts into the animal's skin and then they suck blood. Some ticks can increase their size 20–50 times as they feed. Favorite places for them to locate are between the toes and in the ears, although they can appear anywhere on the skin surface.

A good approach to prevent ticks is to remove underbrush and leaf litter, and to thin the trees in areas where dogs are allowed. This removes the cover and food sources for small mammals that serve as hosts for ticks. Ticks must have adequate cover that provides high levels of moisture and at the same time provides an opportunity of contact with animals. Keeping the lawn well maintained also makes ticks less likely to drop by and stay.

Because of the potential for ticks to transmit a variety of harmful diseases, dogs should be carefully inspected after walks through wooded areas (where ticks may be found), and careful removal of all ticks can be very important in the prevention of disease. Care should be taken not to squeeze, crush, or puncture the body of the tick, since exposure to body fluids of ticks may lead to spread of any disease carried by that tick to the animal or to the person removing the tick. The tick should be disposed of in a container of alcohol or flushed down the toilet. If the site becomes infected, veterinary attention should be sought immediately. Insecticides and repellents should only be applied to pets following appropriate veterinary advice, since indiscriminate use can be dangerous. Recently, a new tick collar has become available which contains amitraz. This collar not only kills ticks, but causes them to retract from the skin within two to three days. This greatly reduces the chances of ticks transmitting a variety of diseases. A spray formulation has also recently been developed and marketed. It might seem that there should be vaccines for all the diseases carried by ticks, but only a Lyme disease (*Borrelia burgdorferi*) formulation is currently available.

MANGE

Mange refers to any skin condition caused by mites. The contagious mites include ear mites, scabies mites, *Cheyletiella* mites and chiggers. Demodectic mange is associated with proliferation of *Demodex* mites, but they are not considered contagious.

The most common causes of mange in dogs are ear mites, and these are extremely contagious. The best way to avoid ear mites is to buy pups from sources that don't have a problem with ear mite infestation. Otherwise, pups readily acquire them when kept in crowded environments in which other animals might be carriers. Treatment is effective if whole body (or systemic) therapy is used, but relapses are common when medication in the ear canal is the only approach. This is because the mites tend to crawl out of the ear canal when medications are instilled. They simply feed elsewhere on the body until it is safe for them to return to the ears.

Scabies mites and *Cheyletiella* mites are passed on by other dogs that are carrying the mites. They are "social" diseases that can be prevented by preventing exposure of your dog to others that are infested. Scabies (sarcoptic mange) has the dubious honor of being the most itchy disease to which dogs are susceptible. Chigger mites are present in forested areas, and dogs acquire them by roaming in these areas. All can be effectively diagnosed and treated by your veterinarian should your dog happen to become infested.

A Cocker with scabies and a secondary bacterial infection.

HEARTWORM

Heartworm disease is caused by the worm *Dirofilaria immitis* and is spread by mosquitoes. The female heartworms produce microfilariae (baby worms) that circulate in the bloodstream, waiting to be picked up by mosquitoes to pass the infection along. Dogs do not get heartworm by socializing with infected dogs; they only get infected by mosquitoes that carry the infective microfilariae. The adult heartworms grow in the heart and major blood vessels and eventually cause heart failure. Fortunately, heartworm is easily prevented by safe oral medications that can be administered daily or on a once-a-month basis. The once-a-month preparations also help prevent many of the common intestinal parasites, such as hookworms, roundworms and whipworms. Prior to giving any preventative medication for heartworm, an antigen test (an immunologic test that detects heartworms) should be performed by a veterinarian since it is dangerous to give the medication to dogs that harbor the parasite. Some experts also recommend a microfilarial test, just to be doubly certain. Once the test results show that the dog is free of heartworms, the preventative therapy can be commenced. The length of time the heartworm preventatives must be given depends on the length of the mosquito season. In some parts of the country, dogs are on preventative therapy year round. Heartworm vaccines may soon be available but the preventatives now available are easy to administer, inexpensive and quite safe.

INTESTINAL PARASITES

The most important internal parasites in dogs are roundworms, hookworms, tapeworms and whipworms. Roundworms are the most common. It has been estimated that 13 trillion roundworm eggs are discharged in dog feces every day! Studies have shown that 75 percent of all pups carry roundworms and start shedding them by three weeks of age. People are infected by exposure to dog feces containing infective roundworm eggs, not by handling pups. Hookworms can cause a disorder known as cutaneous larva migrans in people. In dogs, they are most dangerous to puppies since they latch onto the intestines and suck blood. They can cause anemia and even death when they are present in large numbers. The most common tapeworm is *Dipylidium caninum,* which is spread by fleas. However, another tapeworm (*Echinococcus multilocularis*) can cause fatal disease in people and can be spread to people from dogs. Whipworms live in the lower parts of the intestines. Dogs get whipworms by consuming infective larvae. However, it may be another three months before they start shedding them in their

A picture of adult worms in a dog's heart. A dog can be infected with more than 100 worms that grow nearly 14 inches long. Courtesy of Merck AgVet.

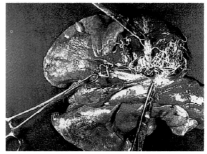

stool, greatly complicating diagnosis. In other words, dogs can be infected by whipworms, but fecal evaluations are usually negative until the dog starts passing those eggs three months after being infected.

Other parasites, such as coccidia, *Cryptosporidium, Giardia,* and flukes can also cause problems in dogs. The best way to prevent all internal parasite problems is to have pups dewormed according to your veterinarian's recommendations, and to have parasite checks done on a regular basis, at least annually.

VIRAL INFECTIONS

Dogs get viral infections such as distemper, hepatitis, parvovirus and rabies by exposure to infected animals. The key to prevention is controlled exposure to other animals and, of course, vaccination. Today's vaccines are extremely effective, and properly vaccinated dogs are at minimal risk for contracting these diseases. However, it is still important to limit exposure to other animals that might be harboring infection. When selecting a facility for boarding or grooming an animal, make sure the staff limits the clientele to animals that have documented vaccine histories. This is in everyone's best interest. Similarly, make sure your veterinarian has a quarantine area for infected dogs and that animals aren't admitted for surgery, boarding, grooming or diagnostic testing without up-to-date vaccinations. By controlling exposure and ensuring vaccination, your pet should be safe from these potentially devastating diseases.

It is beyond the scope of this book to settle all the controversies of vaccination, but they are worth mentioning. Should vaccines be combined in a single injection? It's convenient and cheaper to do it this way, but might some vaccine ingredients interfere with others? Some say yes, some say no. Are vaccine schedules designed for convenience or effectiveness? Mostly convenience. Some ingredients may only need to be given every two or more years. Research is incomplete. Should the dose of the vaccine vary with weight or should a Cocker Spaniel receive the same dose as a Chihuahua or a Great Dane? Good questions, no definitive answers. Finally, should we be using modified live or inactivated vaccine products? There is no short answer for this debate. Ask your veterinarian and do a lot of reading yourself!

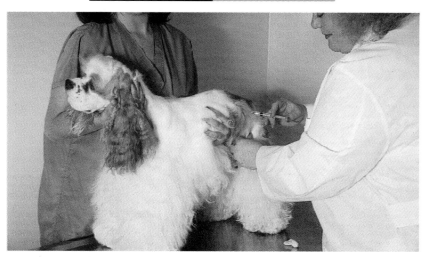

Routine vaccinations will keep your Cocker protected against viral infections such as distemper, rabies and canine cough.

CANINE COUGH

Canine infectious tracheobronchitis, also known as canine cough and kennel cough, is a contagious viral/bacterial disease that results in a hacking cough that may persist for many weeks. It is common wherever dogs are kept in close quarters, such as kennels, pet stores, grooming parlors, dog shows, training classes, and even veterinary clinics. The condition doesn't respond well to most medications, but eventually clears spontaneously over a course of many weeks. Pneumonia is a possible but uncommon complication.

Prevention is best achieved by limiting exposure and utilizing vaccination. The fewer opportunities you give your dog to contact others, the less the likelihood of getting infected. Vaccination is not foolproof because many different viruses can be involved. Parainfluenza virus is included in most vaccines and is one of the more common viruses known to initiate the condition. *Bordetella bronchiseptica* is the bacterium most often associated with tracheobronchitis, and a vaccine is now available that needs to be repeated twice yearly for dogs at risk. This vaccine is squirted into the nostrils to help stop the infection before it gets deeper into the respiratory tract. Make sure the vaccination is given several days (preferably two weeks) before exposure to ensure maximal protection.

FIRST AID   by Judy Iby, RVT

KNOWING YOUR DOG IN GOOD HEALTH

With some experience, you will learn how to give your dog a physical at home, and consequently will learn to recognize many potential problems. If you can detect a problem

early, you can seek timely medical help and thereby decrease your dog's risk of developing a more serious problem.

Facing page: Knowing what healthy teeth and gums look like will help you know when something looks wrong.

Every pet owner should be able to take his pet's temperature, pulse, respirations, and check the capillary refill time (CRT). Knowing what is normal will alert the pet owner to what is abnormal, and this can be life saving for the sick pet.

TEMPERATURE
The dog's normal temperature is 100.5 to 102.5 degrees Fahrenheit. Take the temperature rectally for at least one minute. Be sure to shake the thermometer down first, and you may find it helpful to lubricate the end. It is easy to take the temperature with the dog in a standing position. Be sure to hold on to the thermometer so that it isn't expelled or sucked in. A dog could have an elevated temperature if he is excited or if he is overheated; however, a high temperature could indicate a medical emergency. On the other hand, if the temperature is below 100 degrees, this could also indicate an emergency.

CAPILLARY REFILL TIME AND GUM COLOR
It is important to know how your dog's gums look when he is healthy, so you will be able to recognize a difference if he is not feeling well. There are a few breeds, among them the Chow

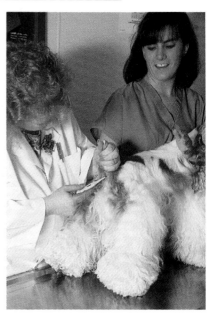

Learn to take your dog's temperature—it's the first thing you should check if your dog's feeling out of sorts.

Chow and its relatives, that have black gums and a black tongue. This is normal for them. In general, a healthy dog will have bright pink gums. Pale gums are an indication of shock or anemia and are an emergency. Likewise, any yellowish tint is an indication of a sick dog. To check capillary refill time (CRT) press your thumb against the dog's gum. The gum will blanch out (turn white) but should refill (return to the normal pink color) in one to two seconds. CRT is very important. If the refill time is slow and your dog is acting poorly, you should call your veterinarian immediately.

HEART RATE, PULSE, AND RESPIRATIONS

Heart rate depends on the breed of the dog and his health. Normal heart rates range from about 50 beats per minute in the larger breeds to 130 beats per minute in the smaller breeds. You can take the heart rate by pressing your fingertips on the dog's chest. Count for either 10 or 15 seconds, and then multiply by either 6 or 4 to obtain the rate per minute. A normal pulse is the same as the heart rate and is taken at the femoral artery located on the insides of both rear legs. Respirations should be observed and depending on the size and breed of the dog should be 10 to 30 per minute. Obviously, illness or excitement could account for abnormal rates.

PREPARING FOR AN EMERGENCY

It is a good idea to prepare for an emergency by making a list and keeping it by the phone. This list should include:
1. Your veterinarian's name, address, phone number, and office hours.
2. Your veterinarian's policy for after-hour care. Does he take his own emergencies or does

he refer them to an emergency clinic?
3. The name, address, phone number and hours of the emergency clinic your veterinarian uses.
4. The number of the National Poison Control Center for Animals in Illinois: 1-800-548-2423. It is open 24 hours a day.

In a true emergency, time is of the essence. Some signs of an emergency may be:
1. Pale gums or an abnormal heart rate.
2. Abnormal temperature, lower than 100 degrees or over 104 degrees.
3. Shock or lethargy.
4. Spinal paralysis.

A dog hit by a car needs to be checked out and probably should have radiographs of the chest and abdomen to rule out pneumothorax or ruptured bladder.

Tying an emergency muzzle.

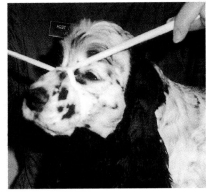

EMERGENCY MUZZLE

An injured, frightened dog may not even recognize his owner and may be inclined to bite. If your dog should be injured, you may need to muzzle him to protect yourself before you try to handle him. It is a good idea to practice muzzling the calm, healthy dog so you understand the technique. Slip a lead over his head for control. You can tie his mouth shut with something like a two-foot-long bandage or piece of cloth. A necktie, stocking, leash or even a piece of rope will also work.

1. Make a large loop by tying a loose knot in the middle of the bandage or cloth.
2. Hold the ends up, one in each hand.
3. Slip the loop over the dog's muzzle and lower jaw, just behind his nose.
4. Quickly tighten the loop so he can't open his mouth.
5. Tie the ends under his lower jaw.
6. Make a knot there and pull the ends back on each side of his face, under the ears, to the back of his head.

If he should start to vomit, you will need to remove the muzzle immediately. Otherwise, he could aspirate vomitus into his lungs.

ANTIFREEZE POISONING

Antifreeze in the driveway is a potential killer. Because antifreeze is sweet, dogs will lap it up. The active ingredient in antifreeze is ethylene glycol, which causes irreversible kidney damage. If you witness your pet ingesting antifreeze, you should call your veterinarian immediately. He may recommend that you induce vomiting at once by using hydrogen peroxide, or he may recommend a test to confirm antifreeze ingestion. Treatment is aggressive and must be administered promptly if the dog is to live, but you wouldn't want to subject your dog to unnecessary treatment.

BEE STINGS

A severe reaction to a bee sting (anaphylaxis) can result in difficulty breathing, collapse and even death. A symptom of a bee sting is swelling around the muzzle and face. Bee stings are antihistamine responsive. It is safest and most effective to contact your veterinarian for recommendations on safe antihistamines and the doses to administer. You should monitor the dog's gum color and respirations and watch for a decrease in swelling. If your dog is showing signs of anaphylaxis, your veterinarian may need to give him an

This puppy's muzzle is swollen from a bee sting.

injection of corticosteroids. It would be wise to call your veterinarian and confirm treatment.

BLEEDING

Bleeding can occur in many forms, such as a ripped dewclaw, a toenail cut too short, a puncture wound, a severe laceration, etc. If a pressure bandage is needed, it must be released every 15-20 minutes. Be careful of elastic bandages since it is easy to apply them too tightly. Any bandage material should be clean. If no regular bandage is available, a small towel or wash cloth can be used to cover the wound and bind it with a necktie, scarf, or something similar. Styptic powder, or even a soft cake of soap, can be used to stop a bleeding toenail. A ripped dewclaw or toenail may need to be cut back by the veterinarian and possibly treated with

antibiotics. Depending on their severity, lacerations and puncture wounds may also need professional treatment. Your first thought should be to clean the wound with peroxide, soap and water, or some other antiseptic cleanser. Don't use alcohol since it deters the healing of the tissue.

BLOAT

Although not generally considered a first aid situation, bloat can occur in a dog rather suddenly. Truly, it is an emergency! Gastric dilatation-volvulus or gastric torsion—the twisting of the stomach to cut off both entry and exit, causing the organ to "bloat," is a disorder primarily found in the larger, more deep-chested breeds. It is life threatening and requires immediate veterinary assistance.

BURNS

If your dog gets a chemical burn, call your veterinarian immediately. Rinse any other burns with cold water and if the burn is significant, call your veterinarian. It may be necessary to clip the hair around the burn so it will be easier to keep clean. You can cleanse the wound on a daily basis with saline and apply a topical antimicrobial ointment, such as silver sulfadiazine 1 percent cream or gentamicin cream. Burns can be debilitating, especially to an older pet. They can cause pain and shock. It takes about three weeks for the skin to slough after the burn and there is the possibility of permanent hair loss.

CARDIOPULMONARY RESUSCITATION (CPR)

Check to see if your dog has a heart beat, pulse and spontaneous respiration. If his pupils are already dilated and fixed, the prognosis is less favorable. This is an emergency situation that requires two people to administer lifesaving techniques. One person needs to breathe for the dog while the other person tries to establish heart rhythm. Mouth to mouth resuscitation starts with two initial breaths, one to one and a half seconds in duration. After the initial breaths, breathe for the dog once after every five chest compressions. (You do not want to expand the dog's lungs while his chest is

Be careful if you put a heating pad in the whelping box—it could burn the puppies' thin skin.

You may be tempted to give your adorable puppy some tasty chocolate, but *don't*. Even in small amounts chocolate can poison a dog.

being compressed.) You inhale, cover the dog's nose with your mouth, and exhale *gently*. You should see the dog's chest expand. Sometimes, pulling the tongue forward stimulates respiration. You should be ventilating the dog 12-20 times per minute. The person managing the chest compressions should have the dog lying on his right side with one hand on either side of the dog's chest, directed over the heart between the fourth and fifth ribs (usually this is the point of the flexed elbow). The number of compressions administered depends on the size of the patient. Attempt 80-120 compressions per minute. Check for spontaneous respiration and/or heart beat. If present, monitor the patient and discontinue resuscitation.

If you haven't already done so, call your veterinarian at once and make arrangements to take your pet in for professional treatment.

CHOCOLATE TOXICOSIS

Dogs like chocolate, but chocolate kills dogs. Its two basic chemicals, caffeine and theobromine, overstimulate the dog's nervous system. Ten ounces of milk chocolate can kill a 12-pound dog. Symptoms of poisoning include restlessness, vomiting, increased heart rate, seizure, and coma. Death is possible. If your dog has ingested chocolate, you can give syrup of ipecac at a dosage of one-eighth of a teaspoon per pound to induce vomiting. Two tablespoons of hydrogen peroxide is an alternative treatment.

CHOKING

You need to open the dog's mouth to see if any object is visible. Try to hold him upside down to see if the object can be dislodged. While you are working on your dog, call your veterinarian, as time may be critical.

DOG BITES

If your dog is bitten, wash the area and determine the severity of the situation. Some bites may need immediate attention, for instance, if it is bleeding profusely or if a lung is punctured. Other bites may be only superficial scrapes. Most dog bite cases need to be seen by the veterinarian, and some may require antibiotics. It is important that you learn if the offending dog has had a rabies vaccination. This is important for your dog, but also for you, in case you are the victim. Wash the wound and call your doctor for further instructions. You should check on your tetanus vaccination history. Rarely, and I mean rarely, do dogs get tetanus. If the offending dog is a stray, try to confine him for observation. He will need to be confined for ten days. A dog that has bitten a human and is not current on his rabies vaccination cannot receive a rabies vaccination for ten days. Dog bites should be reported to the Board of Health.

DROWNING

Remove any debris from the dog's mouth and swing the dog, holding him upside down. Stimulate respiration by pulling his tongue forward. Administer CPR if necessary, and call your veterinarian. Don't give up working on the dog. Be sure to wrap him in blankets if he is cold or in shock.

ELECTROCUTION

You may want to look into puppy proofing your house by installing GFCIs (Ground Fault Circuit Interrupters) on your electrical outlets. A GFCI just saved my dog's life. He had pulled an extension cord into his crate and was "teething" on it at seven years of age. The GFCI kept him from being electro-

These puppies are playing and won't seriously harm each other, but two strange dogs may fight and bite each other.

cuted. Turn off the current before touching the dog. Resuscitate him by administering CPR and pulling his tongue forward to stimulate respiration. Try mouth-to-mouth breathing if the dog is not breathing. Take him to your veterinarian as soon as possible since electrocution can cause internal problems, such as lung damage, which need medical treatment.

EYES

Red eyes indicate inflammation, and any redness to the upper white part of the eye (sclera) may constitute an emergency.

Dogs can develop a number of eye problems; get used to checking your Cocker's eyes for cloudiness or foreign objects.

Squinting, cloudiness to the cornea, or loss of vision could indicate severe problems, such as glaucoma, anterior uveitis and episcleritis. Glaucoma is an emergency if you want to save the dog's eye. A prolapsed third eyelid is abnormal and is a symptom of an underlying problem. If something should get in your dog's eye, flush it out with cold water or a saline eye wash. Epiphora and allergic conjunctivitis are annoying and frequently persistent problems. Epiphora (excessive tearing) leaves the area below the eye wet and sometimes stained. The wetness may lead to a bacterial infection. There are numerous causes (allergies, infections, foreign matter, abnormally located eyelashes and adjacent facial hair that rubs against the eyeball, defects or diseases of the tear drainage system, birth defects of the eyelids, etc.) and the treatment is based on the cause. Keeping the hair around the eye cut short and sponging the eye daily will give relief. Many cases are responsive to medical treatment. Allergic conjunctivitis may be a seasonal problem if the dog has inhalant allergies (e.g., ragweed), or it may be a year 'round problem. The conjunctiva becomes red and swollen and is prone to a bacterial infection associated with mucus accumulation or pus in the eye. Again keeping the hair around the eyes short will give relief. Mild corticosteroid drops or ointment will also give relief. The underlying problem should be investigated.

FISH HOOKS

An imbedded fish hook will probably need to be removed by the veterinarian. More than likely, sedation will be required along with antibiotics. Don't try to remove it yourself. The shank of the hook will need to be cut off in order to push the other end through.

FOREIGN OBJECTS

I can't tell you how many chicken bones my first dog ingested. Fortunately she had a "cast iron stomach" and never suffered the consequences. However, she was always going to the veterinarian for treatment. Not all dogs are so lucky. It is unbelievable what some dogs will take a liking to. I have assisted in surgeries in which all kinds of foreign objects were removed from the stomach and/ or intestinal tract. Those objects included socks, pantyhose, stockings, clothing, diapers, sanitary products, plastic, toys, and, last but not least, rawhides. Surgery is costly and not always successful, especially if it is performed too late. If you see or suspect your dog has ingested a foreign object, contact your veterinarian immediately. He may tell you to induce vomiting or he may have you bring your dog to the clinic immediately. Don't induce vomiting without the veterinarian's permission, since the object may cause more damage on the way back up than it would if you allow it to pass through.

Hard chew toys like the Nylabone® help keep your dog's teeth and gums healthy.

chocolate flavoured

NC-101

NYLABONE

POOCH PACIFIER

SAVES MONEY & DOGS' LIVES

NYLON

Endorsed by LEADING DOG AUTHORITIES and GUARANTEED! ... ASK YOUR VETERINARIAN

PETITE SIZE

"WHY" On Reverse Side !

See Full Guarantee on Reverse Side

NYLABONE® Pooch Pacifier®

Cockers, like all dogs, are prone to heatstroke in the summer months—the only thing better than shade and cool water is air conditioning.

HEATSTROKE

Heatstroke is an emergency! The classic signs are rapid, shallow breathing; rapid heartbeat; a temperature above 104 degrees; and subsequent collapse. The dog needs to be cooled as quickly as possible and treated immediately by the veterinarian. If possible, spray him down with cool water and pack ice around his head, neck, and groin. Monitor his temperature and stop the cooling process as soon as his temperature reaches 103 degrees. Nevertheless, you will need to keep monitoring his temperature to be sure it doesn't elevate again. If the temperature continues to drop to below 100 degrees, it could be life threatening. Get professional help immediately. Prevention is more successful than treatment. Those at the greatest risk are brachycephalic (short nosed) breeds, obese dogs, and those that suffer from cardiovascular disease. Dogs are not able to cool off by sweating as people can. Their only way is through panting and radiation of heat from the skin surface. When stressed and exposed to high environmental temperature, high humidity, and poor ventilation, a dog can suffer heatstroke very quickly. Many people do not realize how quickly a car can overheat. Never leave a dog unattended in a car. It is even against the law in some states. Also, a brachycephalic, obese, or infirm dog should never be left unattended outside during inclement weather and should have his activities curtailed. Any dog left outside, by law, must be assured adequate shelter (including shade) and fresh water.

POISONS

Try to locate the source of the poison (the container which lists the ingredients) and call your veterinarian immediately. Be prepared to give the age and weight of your dog, the quantity of poison consumed and the probable time of ingestion. Your veterinarian will want you to read off the ingredients. If you can't reach him, you can call a local poison center or the National Poison Control Center for Animals in Illinois, which is open 24 hours a day. Their phone number is 1-800-548-2423. There is a charge for their service, so you may need to have a credit card number available.

Symptoms of poisoning include muscle trembling and weakness, increased salivation, vomiting and loss of bowel control. There are numerous household toxins (over 500,000). A dog can be poisoned by toxins in the garbage. Other poisons include pesticides, pain relievers, prescription drugs, plants, chocolate, and cleansers. Since I own small dogs I don't have to worry about my dogs jumping up to the kitchen counters, but when I owned a large breed she would clean the counter, eating all the prescription medications.

Your pet can be poisoned by means other than directly ingesting the toxin. Ingesting a rodent that has ingested a rodenticide is one example. It is possible for a dog to have a reaction to the pesticides used by exterminators. If this is suspected you should contact the exterminator about the potential dangers of the pesticides used and their side effects.

Don't give human drugs to your dog unless your veterinarian has given his approval. Some human medications can be deadly to dogs.

POISONOUS PLANTS

Amaryllis (bulb)	Jasmine (berries)
Andromeda	Jerusalem Cherry
Apple Seeds (cyanide)	Jimson Weed
Arrowgrass	Laburnum
Avocado	Larkspur
Azalea	Laurel
Bittersweet	Locoweed
Boxwood	Marigold
Buttercup	Marijuana
Caladium	Mistletoe (berries)
Castor Bean	Monkshood
Cherry Pits	Mushrooms
Chokecherry	Narcissus (bulb)
Climbing Lily	Nightshade
Crown of Thorns	Oleander
Daffodil (bulb)	Peach
Daphne	Philodendron
Delphinium	Poison Ivy
Dieffenbachia	Privet
Dumb Cane	Rhododendron
Elderberry	Rhubarb
Elephant Ear	Snow on
English Ivy	the Mountain
Foxglove	Stinging Nettle
Hemlock	Toadstool
Holly	Tobacco
Hyacinth (bulb)	Tulip (bulb)
Hydrangea	Walnut
Iris (bulb)	Wisteria
Japanese Yew	Yew

This list was published in the American Kennel Club *Gazette*, February, 1995. As the list states

Know what plants are in your home and yard in case your puppy ingests something bad for him.

these are common poisonous plants, but this list may not be complete. If your dog ingests a poisonous plant, try to identify it and call your veterinarian. Some plants cause more harm than others.

PORCUPINE QUILLS

Removal of quills is best left up to your veterinarian since it can be quite painful. Your unhappy dog would probably appreciate being sedated for the removal of the quills.

SEIZURE (CONVULSION OR FIT)

Many breeds, including mixed breeds, are predisposed to seizures, although a seizure may be secondary to an underlying medical condition. Usually a seizure is not considered an emergency unless it lasts longer than ten minutes. Nevertheless, you should notify your veterinarian. Dogs do not swallow their tongues. Do not handle the dog's mouth since your dog probably cannot control his actions and may inadvertently bite you. The seizure can be mild; for instance, a dog can have a seizure standing up. More frequently the dog will lose consciousness and may urinate and/or defecate. The best thing you can do for your dog is to put him in a safe place or to block off the stairs or areas where he can fall.

Dogs who spend a lot of time outdoors should be checked for things that could harm or injure them, like burrs, scrapes or even skunks.

A healthy, well-cared-for Cocker Spaniel has a contagious *joie de vivre*.

Because puppies are so curious, they need to be watched so they don't get into trouble around the house.

SEVERE TRAUMA

See that the dog's head and neck are extended so if the dog is unconscious or in shock, he is able to breathe. If there is any vomitus, you should try to get the head extended down with the body elevated to prevent vomitus from being aspirated. Alert your veterinarian that you are on your way.

SHOCK

Shock is a life threatening condition and requires immediate veterinary care. It can occur after an injury or even after severe fright. Other causes of shock are hemorrhage, fluid loss, sepsis, toxins, adrenal insufficiency, cardiac failure, and anaphylaxis. The symptoms are a rapid weak pulse, shallow breathing, dilated pupils, subnormal temperature, and muscle weakness. The capillary refill time (CRT) is slow, taking longer than two seconds for normal gum color to return. Keep the dog warm while transporting him to the veterinary clinic. Time is critical for survival.

SKUNKS

Skunk spraying is not necessarily an emergency, although it would be in my house. If the dog's eyes are sprayed, you need to rinse them well with water. One remedy for deskunking the dog is to wash him in tomato juice and follow with a soap and water bath. The newest remedy is bathing the dog in a mixture of one quart of three percent hydrogen peroxide, quarter cup baking soda, and one teaspoon liquid soap. Rinse well. There are also commercial products available.

SNAKE BITES

It is always a good idea to know what poisonous snakes reside in your area. Rattlesnakes, water moccasins, copperheads, and coral snakes are residents of some areas of the United States. Pack ice around the area that is bitten and call your veterinarian immediately to alert him that you are on your way. Try to identify the snake or at least be able to describe it (for the use of antivenin). It is possible that he may send you to another clinic that has the proper antivenin.

TOAD POISONING

Bufo toads are quite deadly. You should find out if these nasty little critters are native to your area.

VACCINATION REACTION

Once in a while, a dog may suffer an anaphylactic reaction to a vaccine. Symptoms include swelling around the muzzle, extending to the eyes. Your veterinarian may ask you to return to his office to determine the severity of the reaction. It is possible that your dog may need to stay at the hospital for a few hours during future vaccinations.

With an appropriate toy like a Nylafloss® to play with, you can be sure your dog won't get hurt or into trouble.

Kathy and Ken Wadley's Ch. Afton's Singing in the Rain is ready for an adventure.

RECOMMENDED READING

DR. ACKERMAN'S DOG BOOKS FROM T.F.H.

OWNER'S GUIDE TO DOG HEALTH
TS-214, 432 pages
Over 300 color photographs

Winner of the 1995 Dog Writers Association of America's Best Health Book, this comprehensive title gives accurate, up-to-date information on all the major disorders and conditions found in dogs. Completely illustrated to help owners visualize signs of illness, different states of infection, procedures and treatment, it covers nutrition, skin disorders, disorders of the major body systems (reproductive, digestive, respiratory), eye problems, vaccines and vaccinations, dental health and more.

SKIN & COAT CARE FOR YOUR DOG
TS-249 224 pages
Over 200 color photographs

Dr. Ackerman, a specialist in the field of dermatology and a Diplomate of the American College of Veterinary Dermatology, joins 14 of the world's most respected dermatologists and other experts to produce an extremely helpful manual on the dog's skin. Coat and skin problems are extremely common in the dog, and owners need to better understand the conditions that affect their dog's coats. The book details everything from the basics of parasites and mange to grooming techniques, medications, hair loss and more.

DOG BEHAVIOR AND TRAINING
Veterinary Advice for Owners
TS-252, 292 pages
Over 200 color photographs

Joined by co-editors Gary Landsberg, DVM and Wayne Hunthausen, DVM, Dr. Ackerman and about 20 experts in behavioral studies and training set forth a practical guide to the common problems owners experience with their dogs. Since behavioral disorders are the number-one reason for owners to abandon a dog, it is essential for owners to understand how the dog thinks and how to correct him if he misbehaves. The book cover socialization, selection, rewards and punishment, puppy-problem prevention, excitable and disobedient behaviors, sexual behaviors, aggression, children, stress and more.

RECOMMENDED READING

COCKER SPANIEL BOOKS FROM T.F.H.

A NEW OWNER'S GUIDE TO COCKER SPANIELS
by Judy Iby
JG-106, 160 pages
over 150 color photographs
For a new or prospective owner of a Cocker Spaniel, this is the perfect book for getting acquainted with this merry breed. There are chapters on selecting the dog for you, characteristics of the Cocker Spaniel, feeding, grooming, housebreaking and training a Cocker, as well as health care. With color photos that jump off the page.

COCKER SPANIELS
by Bart King
KW-043S, 224 pages, all color
Another classic for the novice Cocker Spaniel owner, this handy paperback covers all aspects or raising one of America's all-time favorite breeds.

THE WORLD OF THE COCKER SPANIEL
by Bill Gorodner and Lloyd Alton
TS-198, 624 pages
over 1500 color photographs
See every aspect of owning a Cocker Spaniel come alive in this authoritative and complete manual on the breed. Covering everything from history to genetics to competing in dog shows, obedience, field trials and other activities, this is the ultimate book on the Cocker Spaniel.